My Very Best,

James

QUANTUM LEAP
THINKING

QUANTUM LEAP
THINKING

An Owner's Guide to the Mind

DOVE
BOOKS

ISBN 0-7871-0683-6

Printed in the United States of America

Dove Books
301 North Cañon Drive
Beverly Hills, CA 90210

Distributed by Penguin USA

Text design Stanley S. Drate/Folio Graphic's Co., Inc.

First Printing: March 1996

10   9   8   7   6   5   4   3   2

In memory of my mother, Margaret Madeline Mapes
and
to my father, Earl Steven Mapes,
a lifetime of gratitude

Acknowledgments

This book is a reflection of all those who participated, knowingly and unknowingly, in making a dream into a reality.

■ Susan Granger, friend, lover, and partner, for her patience, skill, and, above all, her time. Her input can be found on every page. Thanks for toting hundreds of pages around on airlines, for correcting my spelling and grammar, and for making me look good.

■ Sherri Daley, my assistant, for her dedication and tenacity and for pushing me to write the book. Her editing skills and willingness to type and retype numerous drafts of this manuscript made this book possible.

■ E. Katherine Kerr, friend and spiritual guide of many years. Part of the original "leaper colony," she helped bring the Quantum Leap Thinking Organization into being by suggesting the name.

■ Tony D'Amelio, dear friend, champion, coach, and lecture agent. His undying faith in me has kept me going through the toughest of times and his feedback has shaped the many incarnations of my corporate programs.

■ Armand Deutsch, Bella Linden, Jack and Richard Lawrence, Ken Williams, Owen and Chris Smith, and my brother, Dave Mapes, for their love and loyalty.

■ Thanks to all those writers and speakers who have influenced my beliefs.

■ Thanks to Lee Montgomery and to all at Dove Books, but especially to Michael Viner for saying yes.

CONTENTS

QUANTUM LEAP THINKING DEFINED

LAYING THE GROUNDWORK

TAKING THE LEAP

BALANCING YOUR LIFE

FROM ME TO WE

PREFACE

When I was thirteen, I earned money by reluctantly mowing the neighbors' lawns. I grumbled and griped, wondering if it was possible to make a living by doing what I really wanted to do: help people create magic in their lives. I loved magic. Magic was my secret and silent partner. Magic is about the imagination. Magic speaks to the deepest part of our souls about possibilities and provides the opportunity to suspend judgment and, simply, believe.

I first developed an interest in magic at age twelve, when I noticed the look of delight on people's faces as they watched magic tricks. People were entranced by the simplest sleight of hand. Although I didn't know it at the time, I was irrevocably hooked on that look of enchantment, and I was already launched on the path I would follow for the next thirty-eight years.

Quantum Leap Thinking is as close to real magic as I've ever seen, yet the development of an entire philosophy and an organization to support it did not happen by accident. Six specific events led me to define a highly effective strategy for success and to become a motivational speaker.

The first was my discovery, through magic, of that look of enchantment; the second was my introduction to the theater.

When I was a junior in high school—rapidly growing, too tall, overweight, and awkward—I was desperately in need of acceptance. I found it in the theater, along with companionship, hard work, discipline, and excitement. Acting stretched my creative spirit. I later went to college to study math and chemistry, but I yearned to act. The joy of bringing words to life seduced me onto the stage, and I spent my college years writing, directing, and producing, as well as designing lights, costumes, and stage sets; because, after all, theater is magic, too.

In 1970 I saw my first stage hypnotist, a man named Sam La-
vine. He did a benefit for a regional theater in New Orleans, where
I was working as an actor. Like the people he brought onstage, I
was mesmerized. While part of me felt that what I was watching
was fake, a stronger part of me was awed and a little frightened.
This was the third event, because if hypnosis was real, it brought
magic to a new level.

In 1972 someone gave me my first self-help book, Napoleon
Hill's *Think and Grow Rich,* the fourth major event. The book
focused on setting clear goals, seeing them as already achieved,
and then setting up an action plan with positive thinking, visualization, and affirmations. I threw myself into the process and it
worked beyond my wildest dreams. Like magic. I became a learning junkie, reading everything I could get my hands on about self-
growth, philosophy, physiology, psychology, and, later, neurology
and quantum physics. I studied Transcendental Meditation and
Silva Mind Control. I took endless self-improvement seminars.

I studied to become a clinical hypnotist. I had to overcome my
own preconceptions about hypnosis, but once I did, it provided
an explanation for how we develop our beliefs, communicate, and
experience reality. I used self-hypnosis to motivate myself to exercise and lose weight. It seemed the perfect tool to help create
and manage changes, an exciting arena in which to push the
boundaries of belief.

As a clinical hypnotist, I learned the power of belief systems,
the dynamics of change, and the elegance of the creative imagination. This, then, was the fifth event, from which the model for
Quantum Leap Thinking emerged. I created an intensive seminar,
"Positive Self-Image Training," which eventually became a workshop called "Choices." Ninety percent of what would eventually
become Quantum Leap Thinking solidified over that period and a
leap took place that changed my life. Quantum Leap Thinking
became a reality and a success beyond my expectations.

I have written this book to share with you a vision that has
worked for me and for many other individuals and organizations.
This book is about changing the way you think, creating a compelling future, and enjoying the process. Quantum Leap Thinking is
a strategy to help you create and maintain a higher quality of life.

When you see a movie, read a novel, watch television, or go to the theater, you suspend your disbelief and focus on the screen, book, or stage. You allow the process to unfold. You may even feel as if you have become part of the story. You may get bored or skeptical, but for the most part, you let the story take on a life of its own. It makes the process enjoyable and fun.

Similarly, major breakthroughs in science and medicine have come from someone simply believing that a new idea has validity. The act of admitting the *possibility* of a solution sets in motion the necessary mental processes to solve the problem.

So as you read this book, pretend that what I say is true. I'm not suggesting that you believe everything I say for the rest of your life; just pretend that it *might* be true—for now.

Suspend your disbelief. Trust that the possibilities are there. You have nothing to lose and everything to gain. Remember Shakespeare's words from *Hamlet*: "There are more things in heaven and earth, Horatio, than are dreamt of in your philosophy."

QLT *THEOREM*

IF YOU THINK THE WAY YOU HAVE ALWAYS THOUGHT AND DO WHAT YOU HAVE ALWAYS DONE, YOU WILL GET THE RESULTS YOU HAVE ALWAYS GOTTEN.

You will notice a number of QLT (Quantum Leap Thinking) Theorems sprinkled throughout the book. Why the word *theorem*? Because until you discover the truth of these simple principles, they will remain only theory, not reality. They are meant to be proven. They are signposts for a personal journey.

Keep a journal as you read. You will want to do the exercises and record your insights and emotions. When you examine your belief systems, you'll have a lot of questions and feel a lot of resistance. You should record all of this in your journal.

Reading this book might be one of the events in your life that create quantum leaps. I had six. Magic instilled in me a desire to enchant. Theater taught me to understand the creative process. Hypnosis opened the door to limitless possibility. My first self-help book lured me into learning. My work as a clinical hypnotist and seminar leader clarified the dynamics of change, belief systems, and the imagination.

But it was the sixth major event that triggered a quantum leap in my life.

In the spring of 1981 I had reached a crisis in my career. For the past eight years I had been traveling, lecturing at colleges and universities, and conducting a series of public seminars in personal growth and visualization.

I was burned out. I was sick far too often and tired all the time. I was functioning, but I was practically unconscious. Then I walked through a plate-glass window in the lobby of a hotel.

That woke me up. I put the brakes on and took a deep breath. I needed to change things, and I needed help to do that, so I invited a group of close friends over for a weekend. Their task was to help me figure out what my vision of the future looked like and to help point me in the direction of my next career move.

I covered the walls of my small apartment with corkboard. Then I wrote out what I thought were my skills and tacked them up on the wall. When my friends got there, we brainstormed about career choices.

We had a lot of fun the first day. Some of our ideas were totally crazy, and some were dull and practical. Nevertheless, we put them all up on the board and had a great time doing it.

The second day was more somber. We talked about everything, from our families to quantum physics. We became analytical and eliminated the impractical and off-the-wall suggestions. Dozens of ideas were reduced to landfill. Then we studied what remained on the corkboard. One of those career choices was corporate speaker, and that, eventually, was what I settled on.

Then we had to decide what I would speak about. The original idea was a program on creative thinking, and, magically, the name *Quantum Leap Thinking* materialized.

Now, years later, there are more than eight topics in my repertoire, I address more than a hundred corporations and universities a year, I have developed a series of audiotapes and videotapes, and I have published two books—a great tribute to my support group, my braintrust, my personal "Quantum Leaper Colony."

While there were plenty of ideas presented to me in that brainstorming session, I chose only the ones that worked for me and then chose the best out of those. My process of selection was based on what I needed at that point in my life.

In the same way I don't expect you to take every idea presented in this book and make it your own. Think of it this way: If I were to cover a giant pole with tar and throw feathers at it, some of the feathers would stick and some wouldn't. The ideas in this book that make a difference to you will be the ones you need to think about at this point in your personal growth. Those will be the feathers that stick.

Reprinted courtesy Omni Magazine 1993.

QUANTUM LEAP
THINKING
DEFINED

WHAT IS
QUANTUM LEAP THINKING?

Quantum leap: any sudden change or advance
in program policy.

*—Webster's Dictionary
of the English Language*

R ed phosphorus and potassium chlorate are stable chemicals
when kept in isolation, but when they are mixed together
and shaken, they explode. There is undeniable energy and a
transformation takes place.

Quantum Leap Thinking, or QLT, is a collection of ideas, concepts, distinctions, and skills that, when combined like active
chemicals, naturally explode in their own way, catapulting you to a
higher level, a level of increased energy, excitement, and options.

QLT cannot be explained in typical linear fashion because the
concepts, like a group of chemicals mixed and interacting, work in
harmony. Together they form a strategy for personal and professional success.

But not success in the traditional sense: QLT is about quality
of life, and when you incorporate the QLT strategy in your daily
life and practice it with commitment, you will experience a personal creative explosion. You will take the quantum leap.

Let's take a simplistic overview of quantum physics, the genesis of Quantum Leap Thinking.

> A quantum leap, no matter how infinitesimal, always makes a sharp break with the past. It is the discontinuous jump of an electron from one orbit to another, with the particle mysteriously leaving no trace of its path. It is the instantaneous collapse of a wave of probabilities into a single real event.
>
> It is the link between two entirely separate locations, events or ideas, that magical moment when the previously inexplicable is suddenly explained, and a radical new theory is born.
>
> —*Science Digest*

I have read hundreds of self-help books on motivation, creativity, positive thinking, and human consciousness. I have explored hypnosis, meditation, and biofeedback. I have attended lectures, rallies, workshops, retreats, and seminars on the human potential for one reason: to be a better person.

The problem was, I didn't notice a difference. I didn't notice a quantum leap.

Then one day, when I was relaxed and quiet, I saw with sudden clarity that there was a difference. I had taken not one quantum leap but many. I hadn't realized it because I was living it. I had been blind to my own changes, so concerned about getting somewhere that I hadn't noticed I had already arrived.

Once I realized that, I noticed my leaps had a pattern. Each leap was bigger than the previous one, each leap had structure, and each was attained by both conscious and unconscious choices. But the most empowering realization of all was that the clearer my vision, the greater the leap.

Since that insight, I have spoken to hundreds of people about their successes, and I am convinced that leaps occur for either individuals or organizations when they employ the same strategy of vision preceding movement.

To understand this more clearly, it is necessary to have a basic understanding of what has come to be known as the "New Physics." Although this area of science is commonly attributed to the work of German physicist Werner Heisenberg (1901–1976), previous research conducted by Danish physicist Niels Bohr, Max Planck, and Albert Einstein also contributed.

Heisenberg challenged classical mechanical physics by showing how traditional ideas about the world had to be abandoned. Motion, at the subatomic level, he claimed, could no longer be described in terms of continuous movement. Through experimentation, he demonstrated that the mere act of observation caused disturbances on the subatomic level; therefore, neither position nor momentum could be measured accurately.

This impossibility of accurately predicting the path of subatomic particles by measuring position and momentum has become known as the Heisenberg Principle of Uncertainty, or the Principle of Indeterminism. If, in fact, the mere act of observing alters what happens on the subatomic level, imagine what this theory means to our perception of everyday reality. This opens up limitless possibilities. For example, Heisenberg said, "The path comes into existence only when we observe it." In other words, the observer takes part in the actual creation of the path.

To have a universe that depends on the observer is both exciting and disturbing. Does the universe change every time we alter how we view it? Does how we look at something influence our choices? In the subatomic world of the electron it does.

If, just for fun, we choose to relate everything we see and do within the context of quantum physics, we can take the position that we construct reality at every moment of our lives. We choose, consciously or unconsciously, among the many options constantly offered to us.

> Thus, at the quantum level of reality, when we choose to "see" what we see, reality becomes both paradoxical and sensible at the same time. Our acts of observation are what we experience as the everyday world.
>
> —FRED ALAN WOLF,
> *Taking the Quantum Leap*

For example, examine the figure below:

Is this line concave or convex?

As you can see, it all depends on how you look at it. Whatever choice you make is correct and can be justified. *You* create reality. You decide how you're going to look at the line, and your choice determines whether the line is concave or convex.

In fact, you create reality *all the time* by the choices you make.

When measuring light, Heisenberg demonstrated that both the momentum and the position of an atom are potentially present, but not actually present until the attempt is made to measure them. The very act of observation determines whether the wave length (momentum) side of reality or the particle (location) side of reality appears.

"*Actually, the job calls for someone who is convex.*"

QLT *THEOREM*

WHAT IS HIDDEN IN OUR CHOICES IS POTENTIALLY PRESENT.

We shape our information by choice. What we don't choose becomes invisible. When we choose one opportunity, other possibilities move to the background. Thus we alter our reality all the time. The things we do not choose are a potential reality.

> The concept that events are not determined in the peremptory manner, but that the possibility or "tendency" for an event to take place has a kind of reality halfway between the massive reality of matter and the intellectual reality of the idea or image. . . . This concept plays a decisive role in Aristotle's philosophy. In modern quantum theory, this concept takes on a new form: it is formulated . . . as probability and subjected to . . . laws of nature.
> —WERNER HEISENBERG,
> German physicist

This potential reality is available to all of us if we master the skills necessary to "see" all the options available and then make the most empowering choice. Paradigm shifting is a matter of choosing to create a new reality out of what we believe to be true.

The challenge becomes apparent when we realize that the choices we make are the result of the way we look at life, often the result of what we have been told is true. We view life through a filter of belief systems. The composition of that filter determines the quality of our choices, and the clarity of the filter depends on many things, the strongest of which is fear.

Like petroleum jelly on the lens of a camera, fear distorts. We need to clean the lens through which we view life; we need to change our filter. If we are unaware of our power to do that, we become victims. We believe we are powerless—that people, things, or situations are doing things to us.

The first step toward taking a quantum leap is to be willing to examine the filter of your own belief systems.

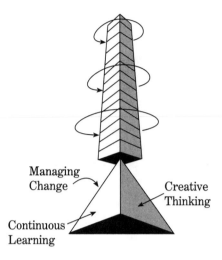

The Quantum Leap Thinking process can be diagrammed as a three-dimensional triangle, base down, on top of which is balanced a rectangle of fourteen sections which are the fourteen points of Quantum Leap Thinking. The skyscraper-like rectangle spins like a top, perfectly balanced on the point of the triangle.

The planes of the triangle on which everything else is built make up the foundation of QLT. Each of the three sides is composed of a survival skill that must be in place and meticulously maintained before the rectangle can spin. These skills are Continuous Learning, Creative Thinking, and Managing Change.

CONTINUOUS LEARNING

Study, learn, but guard the original naiveté. It has to be within you, as desire for drink is within the drunkard or love is within the lover.

—HENRI MATISSE,
French painter

I have always thought that my formal education was a bust. I disliked most of my classes, not because of the subject matter, but because of how they were taught. I hated learning. I hated hearing, "Memorize such-and-such. We'll have a quiz tomorrow."

I confess, I cheated. I cheated because the answers to the questions had already been supplied, and I was very clever at figuring out ways to have those answers available to me. I was inspired to learn new, creative ways of cribbing. If I could find the answers and simply regurgitate them, why should I do more?

True learning is more than response to stimulus, more than a rote answer to a question. Learning is a multilayered and interconnected process that flows among three areas that are separate but connected to one another, forming what I call a Trinity for Learning:

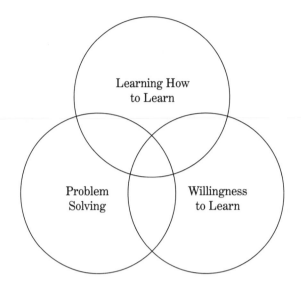

Learning How
to Learn

Problem
Solving

Willingness
to Learn

Problem solving is the most obvious form of learning and vitally important. Solving problems is what I remember most about my formal education. You are probably fairly proficient at this skill, but problem solving is not the part of the learning process that will impact your life. It is within the **Willingness to Learn** circle that you find the potential for personal growth.

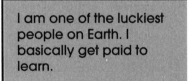

I am one of the luckiest people on Earth. I basically get paid to learn.

Willingness to learn presupposes both a desire and a commitment to step into the unknown. It requires the understanding that learning is a never-ending, ongoing process. It requires a commitment to experience life to the fullest, day by day, moment by moment.

> The true self is always in motion like music, a river of life, changing, moving, failing, suffering, learning, shining.
>
> —BRENDA UELAND,
> *If You Want to Write*

The **Learning How to Learn** loop is pivotal. Real learning is about life, not classroom behavior. What takes place in the classroom must create a foundation for a lifetime of learning, yet even the best classroom training doesn't include the basic principles of creating personal vision, thinking creatively, or managing change.

Charles Handy, London School of Business professor and business consultant, wrote a wonderful book called *The Age of Unreason*. In it he talks about reinventing education and the need for continuous learning in a time of unreasonable change: "Those who are always learning are those who can ride the winds of change and who see a changing world as full of opportunities rather than dangers."

Based on Handy's writing, I present to you an expanded definition of learning:

1. Learning is solving your own problems for your own reasons.
2. Learning is knowing more than just prescribed answers; it is developing curiosity.
3. Learning is more than studying or being trained. Learning is a way of thinking.
4. Learning is a starting point and does not have an end point. Learning is ongoing, a habit, a process.
5. Learning is a methodology that requires thought, courage, energy, commitment, and support.

Certainly we learn by solving problems, but real learning begins with questions: What do I want to create? Who am I? What is my purpose? How does this work? How do I create a recipe? How do I get what I want?

> There is no shortcut to life. To the end of our day, life is a lesson imperfectly learned.
>
> —HARRISON E. SALISBURY,
> *New York Times* reporter

QLT *THEOREM*

LEARNING CAN BE A LIFETIME PROCESS ONLY WHEN THE CIRCLE OF LEARNING IS IN CONTINUOUS MOTION.

▓ THE CIRCLE OF LEARNING

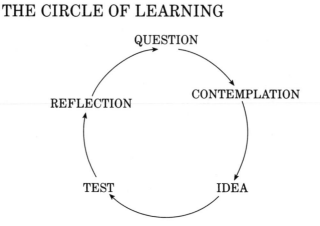

Kids are fascinated with asking questions, but the question stage is supposed to be part of a process, not an end in itself. Children often get stuck in the question mode. They ask questions and happily accept the answers. Some grown-ups are like that, too.

When that happens, learning stops. We're supposed to think about those answers. Contemplation provides a pause in which we generate our next move: the idea.

> Never, never rest contented with any circle of ideas, but always
> be certain that a wider one is still possible.
>> —RICHARD JEFFERIES,
>> nineteenth-century English author

The idea stage provides excitement for experimentation and exploration, but danger lurks here, too. The danger is accepting the idea as fact without asking further questions. An even greater danger is when the idea (usually someone else's) is taught as fact without allowing the possibility of another point of view.

The next stage is the test. It takes courage to test your ideas because you must be willing to have them fail.

Reflection is integral to the process, but overreflection can get you stuck. If we become comfortable with rethinking our ideas, the Circle of Learning grinds to a halt.

True learning is constantly adding to and even changing the way we view the world. Learning is proactive; we are in charge of creating our own destiny.

Education and training are the most important investments we can make in shaping our destiny. *Fortune* magazine has noted again and again that those who survive in the workforce are the individuals who have taken responsibility for their careers, and in order to be responsible for your career, you must take responsibility for your learning. No one is going to do that for you.

> To secure ourselves against defeat lies in our own hands.
>
> —SUN TZU,
> sixth-century Chinese military leader
> and author of *The Art of War*

▓ THE CYCLE OF DISCOVERY

Learning is a never-ending cyclical process of discovery. We uncover possibilities within ourselves, transform them into reality, and discover new possibilities again. Following are the four levels of the cycle, listed from lowest to highest.

Level 4: You don't know you don't know.

This is the lowest level in the Cycle of Discovery. You are unaware of anything but what you believe to be true. You can't see possibilities. For you, possibility does not exist.

Level 3: You know you don't know.

This level can be the stimulus to self-motivation or a mind-set for defeat. It depends on how you decide to think. Are you embarrassed and defensive when you discover your lack of knowledge, or are you intrigued and excited?

Q LT *THEOREM*

TURNING JUDGMENT INTO CURIOSITY OPENS THE CHANNEL FOR LEARNING.

I inherited a family with my second marriage, and the opportunity of watching a child grow in his first three years of life. David's curiosity is astonishing. There is no judgment. He dives in, fearless of the consequences of his investigations.

When I was practicing clinical hypnosis, my specialty was age regression, a process that places the subject in a deep hypnotic state, taking him or her back to that special time of nonjudgmental, fearless curiosity.

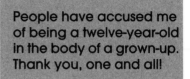

People have accused me of being a twelve-year-old in the body of a grown-up. Thank you, one and all!

In demonstrations of age regression, people re-create childhood handwriting, draw childish pictures, and relive details of their lives with uncanny exactness. Some people speak languages they haven't uttered in years and have long since forgotten. These demonstrations show that the "child" still exists within us, along with our ability to be childlike. The "child within" may have been injured, scarred, or suppressed en route to adulthood, but it's still there.

It is natural to judge. Judgment is our way of making sense out of the information with which we are constantly bombarded. And that judgment comes out of the way we view reality, our paradigm of what we believe to be true.

Making the choice to turn judgment into curiosity is the leap that moves us to the next level in the Cycle of Discovery.

> Be humble, for the worst thing in the world is of the same stuff
> as you; be confident, for the stars are of the same stuff as you.
> —NICHOLAI VELIMIROVICH,
> *The Life of St. Sava*

Level 2: You know you know.

The danger in this level is trying too hard instead of letting go and trusting. You can assume a veneer of arrogance and pretense, like an actor who has memorized his or her lines but is still not believable because there is effort in his or her performance.

I have met many people who become instant preachers after some intensive workshop of self-exploration. They expound with their newly acquired vocabulary and wallow in their newly discovered truths. They feel they have found *the* answer and they want to share it with everyone.

There is nothing wrong with their enthusiasm, but what they have not yet discovered is that they are like the actor who hasn't fully stepped into his or her role.

Level 1: You don't know you know.

Through practice, an actor becomes his or her character. The actor doesn't know he or she knows the lines, because he or she has *become* the character. After a child learns to walk, the child never needs to think about the process. And when you are living your vision, you become your vision. How would you know if you have *become*?

Success, however, can often be the kiss of death because it breeds complacency. Comfort can lead to stagnation. Then, suddenly, what had appeared as success becomes boring. Passion gives way to emptiness, and life seems to be without purpose. To avoid that, you need to keep the Cycle of Discovery in motion.

> As long as you're green, you're growing; as soon as you're ripe, you start to rot.
>
> —RAY KROC,
> founder of McDonald's

What is the total when you divide 30 by ½ and add 10? What answer did you get: 25 or 70? If your answer was 25, you answered a different question and divided 30 by 2, not by ½. The answer to the question as it is precisely posed is 70. Thirty divided by ½ is 60. Add 10 and you have 70.

Quantum Leap Thinking is not really about the answers; it is about questions and how the questions are asked.

▒ INTERACTIVE LEARNING

According to *Fortune,* the world of business is changing fundamentally. The cover article of the May 17, 1994, issue presents six trends that will shape the workplace, and four of these refer to a restructuring of the traditional hierarchy into a "spider's web," or network of specialists and/or technicians. Already more than half of American businesses employ fewer than one hundred people. The majority of companies have fewer than four hundred employees, and the fastest growing segment of American business is the entrepreneur. Home offices are springing up everywhere; *freelance* and *consulting* no longer mean "unemployed." We have become individual members of an enormous corporation: the American business world.

With fewer monolithic companies to act as models, we must learn from one another, a skill I like to call "interactive learning." Instead of looking above for the direction, we will be learning more from the man or woman at our global shoulder.

But a flat organizational structure has a distinctive drawback: There is no obvious leader. In fact, there is the disquieting thought that we all may be leaders.

QLT *THEOREM*

IN OUR OWN WAY, WE ARE ALL LEADERS.

The truth is, we *are* all leaders. Interactive learning is the process by which we learn from one another. Interactive learning is not only the best way, it is the only way we are going to succeed. Unlike learning under the guidance of teachers, parents, or management, interactive learning is self-perpetuating. Like a solar panel, it makes use of the elements, and the elements never go away. We are the elemental pieces that make up the whole of our education.

Interactive learning is the technological wave of the future. Already there are computerized television programs in which we are not viewers but participants. We interact directly with the screen. Our input becomes part of the whole. We create as well as participate. Technology allows us to choose our own endings in interactive feature films. Children create entire stories on personal computers. The options for interactive learning and interactive participation are endless.

I learn from my audiences, so much so that I have recently designed a program that throws the presentation back into their laps. The participants guide the program to an outcome that they have helped create.

What better way to give my clients what they want than to ask them to help me give it to them? Their questions make me think about answers I hadn't verbalized before, and their answers come from a new perspective. At standard question-and-answer periods, I find myself taking notes.

Interaction breeds perspective, respect, and self-confidence, all requisites for creativity. It establishes a feeling of mutual support where participants feel comfortable taking risks, offering new ideas, and abandoning tired, safe, out-of-date beliefs. But the most staggering advantage of interactive learning is the wealth of knowledge we have to play with.

> Trust only movement. Life happens at the level of events not of words. Trust movement.
> —ALFRED ADLER,
> Austrian psychiatrist

CREATIVE THINKING

The future belongs to those who believe in dreams.
—ELEANOR ROOSEVELT,
humanitarian and diplomat

A tiny speck appears on the horizon. It's hard to see. It begins to move closer and closer. It looks like a shapeless blob, but as it moves closer, it starts to take form. The form becomes real, and unexpectedly you are suddenly within the form. The memory of the creation fades because you are now part of the form itself. This is your reality and it is continually growing and shifting.

And then another speck appears on the horizon. . . .

This is the essence of the creative mind. Something appears where nothing previously existed, then takes form and becomes real.

There are countless definitions of creativity. But the process of creative thinking is simply the ability to see something not seen before, bringing something new out of a rearrangement of the old. The destruction of the old gives birth to the new.

Creativity is first of all an act of destruction.
—PABLO PICASSO,
Spanish painter and sculptor

We are all creative. Creative potential is human nature. Some of us may have more highly developed creative skills than others, some may not view themselves as creative types and never try anything they consider "creative," but my guess is that most people have never had anyone show them how to stay out of their own way. I have some practical advice for creative idea generation, and I offer them here to help you remove the stumbling blocks to your own creativity.

Q L T **CREATIVE ADVICE**

BREAK OUT OF THE INTELLIGENCE TRAP.

> Logic is a tool invented for certain uses; it is not the way we deal with reality most of the time, despite our conditioning.
> —MORTON HUNT,
> *The Universe Within*

Many of us believe that intelligence alone should be able to solve problems in both our personal and business relationships. This has led us to believe that innovation, problem solving, productivity, and open communication can be handled by using our brains. The result is the Intelligence Trap: frustration, confusion, guilt, blame, and anxiety.

Creative thinking and logic are really two sides of the same coin; the balance between the two is the mark of a Quantum Leap Thinker.

> The action of the child inventing a new game with his playmates; Einstein formulating a theory of relativity; the housewife devising a new sauce for the meat; a young author writing his first novel; all of these are, in terms of our definition, creative, and there is no attempt to set them in some order of more or less creative.
> —CARL R. ROGERS,
> *On Becoming a Person*

Curiously, people hesitate to recognize the breakthroughs in their own lives as creative acts. If I ask an audience to name people they view as creative, they invariably list famous artists or inventors. No one has ever said, "Me."

Perhaps this reluctance stems from our perception that creative acts must result in something artistic, like a book, a painting, music, or a scientific breakthrough. Or perhaps we have a negative perception of how creative people behave, think, or look.

Have you ever felt the elation that comes with solving a problem, when the answer just came to you? It seemed to go beyond logic. This is creativity, and it occurs more often than you realize. We are creative by nature. Accept the possibility that you are creative, and magic will happen.

QLT *THEOREM*

IF YOU ARE STUCK IN YOUR EGO, YOU LOSE YOUR CREATIVITY.

The creative side of your nature includes intuition, ideas, dreams, fantasy, and invention. Without the creative side of your brain, intelligence is a rather useless tool. Your creative side is elusive and delicate. Fear and negativity can send the creative self into hiding.

The creative mind needs constant nurturing. There is a tremendous payoff to paying attention to the creative side of your being, because only by using your imagination can you shift paradigms and bring forth the invisible.

> Creative ideas come to the intuitive person who can face up to
> the insecurity of looking beyond the obvious.
> —MORTON HUNT,
> *The Universe Within*

QLT *CREATIVE ADVICE*

CREATE SPACE.

> If your mind is empty, it is always ready for anything; it is open
> to everything. In the beginner's mind there are many possibilities; in the expert's mind there are few.
> —SHUNRYU SUZUKI,
> *Zen Mind, Beginner's Mind*

If you have a full glass of water, you can't add anything. Pour some out, and you have room for more. Your mind is much the same. Making space allows the creative mind to add new ideas.

I know that you can justify your "busy-ness." One of the great gifts of the human mind is to create reasons for why we do what we do. That's a creative act, too. But being busy does not necessarily mean being creative or productive.

You probably feel guilty at the thought of taking time off, but guilt is just another form of fear to conquer. There are people who can easily take time for themselves, contemplate, or meditate without letting the "shoulds" creep in. I am not one of them. It takes a real commitment on my part to schedule alone time, but I make the time because I have learned the payoff is always beyond my expectations. I give myself full permission to change my mind and go back to my "schedule," but I seldom do.

If you want to develop your creative thinking ability, schedule stop time. You need the space to grow. I'm not advising you to go off to an ashram, although some people may make that choice. Choose a style of stop time that fits your lifestyle. For me it's daily meditation. For you it may mean twenty minutes of time alone one day a week. If your wife, husband, or significant other is supportive, you may be able to take a week for yourself every six months. When you put the brakes on, you are forced to confront yourself. Busy-ness is often an unconscious choice to avoid reflection.

Q L T *CREATIVE ADVICE*

DO SOMETHING TOTALLY DIFFERENT.

> In inner creativity, the quantum jump allows us to break from established patterns of behavior, which make up what is known as character—what we have become as a result of our years of growing up, our conditioning.
> —AMIT GOSWAMI, Ph.D.,
> *Quantum Mechanics*

Breaking routine is mandatory for the creative process. Go to the opera if you gravitate toward sports. Go to a ball game if you usually go to the theater. Read a biography if you usually read fiction, or poetry if you read only the newspaper. Find a way to break your old ways and shift your patterns of behavior.

I have come up with incredible ideas while flying a kite. You may simply choose to drive a different route to work or eat a different type of food. Go rafting. Go fishing. Walk in a mall. Consciously break your routine. Make yourself a little uncomfortable.

Q LT *THEOREM*

IF YOU CAN'T SEE THE POSSIBILITY, THAT DOESN'T MEAN IT DOESN'T EXIST.

Look at the figure below. What do you see?

Shift your perception. Bring the background to the foreground. You'll see a knight riding a horse. That is what doing something out of the ordinary gives you: a different perspective. By changing the way you look at things, you bring the background to the foreground; you bring forth unseen possibilities.

If you're involved in "keeping up" with life on a day-to-day basis, whether it's handling business or raising children, you may feel exhausted and busy, but you can always do *something* different. Think about it. See if you can come up with four ideas for changing your routine.

Q LT **CREATIVE ADVICE**

CHALLENGE ASSUMPTIONS.

Below is the Roman numeral nine. I want you to make a six out of it.

I X

If you were able to do it, good for you. Most people assume the number can't be tampered with, but the solution is simple. You can add an S in front. Or you can draw a horizontal line through the middle of the Roman numeral, hold it up to a mirror, and look at the top half.

Did you assume that the Roman numeral couldn't be added to or that you couldn't use props? Your assumption stopped possibility. How many opportunities have you missed because you have made an assumption?

Q LT *THEOREM*

ASSUMPTIONS ARE THE DEATH OF POSSIBILITY.

Here are some of the most obvious assumptions. Do any of them sound familiar?

1. My values are your values.
2. You know what I want of you without my asking.
3. I know what you want of me without your telling me.
4. Because something is important to you, it should be considered important by me.
5. My way is the right way and the only way.
6. My understanding of a term or word is your understanding

(i.e., quality, customer service, empowerment, love, selfish, commitment).

7. Things will never change.
8. You know what makes someone else feel loved by knowing what makes you feel loved.
9. My rules for friendship or relationship are your rules for friendship or relationship.
10. I am powerless and cannot make a difference.
11. Things must be done a certain way because that's the way they have always been done.

> The reasonable man adapts himself to the world; the unreasonable man persists in trying to adapt the world to himself. Therefore all progress depends on the unreasonable man.
>
> —GEORGE BERNARD SHAW,
> playwright

I have worked with corporations whose top management knows only one way of doing things. They distrust outsiders, dislike conflict, and cling to their traditional philosophy. In the most negative sense, the entire corporation has become one collective way of thinking. Their collective noses are stuck in a knothole. They have become too comfortable to challenge assumptions, explore new possibilities, encourage risk taking, or check out the facts—like this old story:

> Mom was preparing a Christmas ham for cooking. Her son noticed that she cut off the ends of the ham before placing it in the roasting pan and asked, "Mom, why did you cut off the ends of the ham?"
>
> Never having thought about it much, she replied, "I don't know. Mother always did it that way."
>
> So the young boy sought out his grandmother and asked her why she cut off the ends of the ham before putting it in the oven.
>
> "I don't know," the grandmother answered. "Mother did it that way. Why don't you go ask your great-grandma? She's a little hard of hearing, so you'll have to speak up."
>
> The boy went over to his great-grandmother and in a very

loud voice told her that both his mother and his grandmother always cut the ends off their Christmas ham. "Do you know why?" the boy bellowed.

With a twinkle in her eye, his great-grandmother replied, "I don't know why your mother cuts off the ends of her ham, but I did it because the only roasting pan we owned was too small!"

Peter Drucker writes in his book *Post-Capitalist Society*:

> Every business, in fact every organization, operates on . . . a set of assumptions regarding the outside (customer, markets, distributive channels, competition) and a set of assumptions regarding the inside (core competencies, technology, products, process). These assumptions are usually taken for holy writ by the company and its executives. It is on them that they base their decisions, their actions, their behavior.

Eventually theory becomes inappropriate to the realities of the market and technology. Because of inevitable and rapid change, challenging assumptions must be an ongoing process.

Without rethinking our behavior, rules, and strategies, any attempt to create a vision of possibilities can only result in failure or mediocrity. Consider the Swiss watchmakers who turned down the technology of the digital watch or the record companies who failed to anticipate the compact disc.

Take five minutes and list some assumptions about your children, your spouse, your friends, your relationships, your government, your talents, and your business. Now look them over and decide how many of them are really fact.

You may be surprised; you may even feel a little uncomfortable. And if you have come from the mind-set that your way is the only way, it may be hard to accept that you might have assumed incorrectly.

> Nothing is impossible; there are ways that lead to everything, and if we had sufficient will we should always have sufficient means. It is often merely for an excuse that we say things are impossible.
>
> —FRANÇOIS DE LA ROCHEFOUCAULD,
> fifteenth-century moralist and author of
> *Réflexions on Sentences et Maximes Morales*

IF YOU BELIEVE SOMETHING IS IMPOSSIBLE, YOU HAVE BEFORE YOU A SIGNPOST TO THE POSSIBLE.

▓ FIRE WALKING: A QUANTUM LEAP OF FAITH

In 1973, on an eighty-nine-day cruise around the world, I met a very special person. He was Bruce (Tolly) Burkan, the ship's magician. I had been hired to design and direct theatrical productions on the cruise ship.

When the ship docked in India, Bruce rushed off to spend time with a guru by the name of Si Baba. Upon his return, he told me stories of miracles. He read passages to me from the *Tibetan Book of the Dead.* He introduced me to a life-enhancing work entitled *A Course in Miracles.* I thought he was pretty strange, but after the cruise, we kept in touch.

Years later I learned that Bruce had become a celebrity in Sweden teaching fire walking. He sent me photos. One showed Bruce apparently walking across flaming cinders, and another was a picture of him leading someone else across the hot coals. I was skeptical. What was the trick?

Six months later he returned to his home in a remote part of upstate California. (Where else would someone live who taught fire walking?) He phoned me in New Jersey and informed me that he was going to be presenting the first fire-walking workshop ever given in the United States. There would be about forty participants, and I was welcome to join the group. He assured me the experience would be of great value in all aspects of my life.

What made me even more uncomfortable than the thought of walking on fire was the language he was using—vision, empowerment, personal power, breakthrough, and creating reality. I wasn't familiar with the terminology and the mere thought of revealing my innermost self in public made me feel not only uncomfortable but threatened.

I told Bruce that I was giving a lecture that day. Years later he told me that he knew I was lying; he could hear the fear in my voice. Nevertheless, he wouldn't take no for an answer, so reluctantly I agreed to go.

The workshop was to take place at some "touchy-feely" nature retreat, yet another reason I didn't want to go. I tried to get a friend to go with me, but he didn't take the bait. So off I went. Alone.

I deliberately tried to be late, but I didn't quite succeed. I arrived at the retreat in plenty of time and was directed to a small cabin in the woods.

I was greeted by an unexpected cast of characters. There were six people from the military in full uniform; eleven senior managers, including two CEOs from Fortune 500 companies; several scientists; and a couple of educators and doctors. The group consisted of thirty-six men and four women. Everyone was dressed very formally except me.

The cabin had a dirt floor. There was a flip chart and forty sawed-off tree stumps that served as stools to sit on. Thirty-nine stumps were occupied. I sat on the fortieth.

Bruce entered the room. He had shaved his head bald and was wearing what appeared to be a dress. I silently prayed he would not say hello to me.

Gazing at the group with love and self-confidence, he said, "I know what you're all thinking."

I *still* seriously doubt if he could ever have imagined what we were thinking at that moment.

"This workshop is not just about walking on fire," he went on. "This experience is to be a metaphor for your life. You will discover how your thoughts influence your actions and how, in turn, those actions affect other people. You will learn how to pay attention, create a vision for breakthrough thinking, and turn fear into power."

For years I had worked as a clinical hypnotist and dealt with people on a deeply therapeutic level. I had developed and facilitated several workshops on self-esteem and personal growth. I knew then and I am certain now that what primarily keeps people from going to their next highest level is fear. What intrigued me was Bruce's concept of turning fear into power.

For almost three hours we were lectured to and shown demonstrations about the power of the mind. Then abruptly Bruce announced that we were going outside to build a fire.

There was a sudden shift in attitude. The makings of a team

began to take shape. He guided us as a group to a woodshed, where each of us picked up a bundle of wood and deposited it where we were directed. Bruce splashed the pile of wood with something flammable and threw in a match.

Whoosh! The pile of wood exploded into flame.

Wow, I thought. *That's real.*

I knew at that moment that, like me, everyone was confronted by reality.

We went back into the cabin and, for the next hour or so, while the fire burned, we played some more mind games. First we were told we could walk across hot coals, then we were presented with pictures of failure. Then we were reunited with the positive.

After a while Bruce told us to prepare ourselves. "I want you all to remove your shoes and socks," he instructed. "Gentlemen should roll up their pants legs. If your clothes come within a foot and a half or less of the fire, they will burst into flame." He glanced at us. "We don't want that, do we?"

At that moment everyone in the room regressed. We became scared, excited children. He led us, barefoot, out to the fire and told us to stand in a circle. Standing in the center of the clearing with a rake, Bruce requested we all hold hands.

That was my first truly uncomfortable moment. Holding hands with a group of strangers is not my idea of fun, and it was even less fun for some other people in the group.

Bruce looked around the circle and said, "Now we are going to chant."

Holding hands is uncomfortable enough, but chanting really makes me feel foolish.

"And here's the chant we're going to do," he continued. " 'Open up your mind. See what you find. Bring it on home to your people.' "

Picture, if you will, forty resistant adults, holding hands while standing barefoot around a fire and reluctantly mumbling, "Open up your mind. See what you find. Bring it on home to your people."

Eventually we got into the spirit, partly because the chant had a rhythm to it, but mainly because it went on for nearly an hour.

Bruce picked up the rake and moved toward the fire. It was so hot he had to reach out, using the rake as an extension of his arm, to avoid the intense heat. He knocked off one partially burning log and then another. As he was raking, we were chanting; and I was making my first mistake: I was *observing*. Instead of being totally absorbed in the process, I was being a spectator, judging and letting my thoughts overwhelm me.

Within minutes I noticed that a significant number of our group had taken a little mind-vacation. Their eyeballs rolled back and they were chanting away. "Open up your mind. See what you find. . . ." And so forth.

Bruce finished raking out a bed of coals that seemed to go on forever but was, in reality, approximately twenty feet long and two feet wide. Putting down his rake, he clapped his hands and pulled us back to attention. "I'm going to walk first," he declared. "When the spirit moves you, you can walk." He raised his arms. "Now chant." And chant we did.

What followed was the most powerful sight I have ever seen. Bruce stepped to the edge of the hot coals, calmly focused his attention somewhere in the distance, lifted up his caftan, and walked, slowly and deliberately, across the burning coals. He stepped off, crossed his arms, and waited.

No one moved. No spirits were moving anyone to walk on that fire.

My mind was racing a mile a minute. I knew I had to walk because I had told everyone I knew that I was going to walk on fire. So the question was not "if," but "when?"

I determined to wait until fifteen people had walked. If they made it without screaming and running off into the woods, I would do it. Waiting for twenty to walk would make me a bit of a wimp, but fifteen made sense. I could still tell everyone I was one of the first.

No one moved. I was suddenly reexperiencing past events of my life when I didn't have the courage to act. I made a decision: This would be my personal breakthrough. I would walk . . . third.

I waited. Still no one moved. Time crept by and I suddenly did something incredibly spontaneous. Some may even call it stupid. A little voice in my head screamed, "GO FOR IT!" I jumped out of the circle and stopped in front of the pathway of hot coals.

Let me tell you the difference between fear and terror. You can still function with fear; terror paralyzes you. As I stared at the red-hot coals, one thought kept repeating over and over: "I'm going to burn myself. I'm going to burn myself."

Then my attention shifted to the trees. I realized I had been holding my breath. That's what terror does. I started talking to myself: "Okay, Mapes, get yourself together. Breathe. You teach this to people. Use your stuff."

I looked at the coals again. *I'm going to burn myself.* Then I tried to employ what can be the greatest joke of the human mind . . . positive thinking.

I'll tell you a secret. Positive thinking does not work for negative thinkers. It only makes them feel guilty. Positive thinking works for positive thinkers. Try telling a negative thinker to look at the water glass as half full instead of half empty, or to make lemonade out of lemons. Try telling that to a negative thinker who has just lost his or her job after thirty years or has just had some personal tragedy, and you may just get a black eye.

> Get action. Do things; be sane, don't fritter away your time . . .
> take a place wherever you are and be somebody; get action.
>
> —THEODORE ROOSEVELT,
> twenty-sixth president of the United States

Standing there, I remembered something Bruce had drilled into us throughout the workshop. "See yourself already across the fire. See yourself already where you want to be." Very simple. At that moment I *was* able to see myself across the coals and on the other side. I launched forth.

I remember only the first two steps, and admittedly they were warm. Suddenly I was on cool grass. I had done it. I had walked on fire.

I felt a powerful emotion welling up within me and I burst into tears. It was the release of all that tension.

That twenty-foot walk was an incredible experience for me. Not just because it was possible, but because I had really believed it was impossible.

This experience changed my definition of "impossible" forever. My ability to walk on hot coals implanted a mechanism deep in my subconscious, a mechanism that, from time to time when needed, reminds me to challenge my assumptions.

QLT CREATIVE ADVICE

CREATE A POWER GROUP.

Remember the self-help book I referred to in the preface, Napoleon Hill's *Think and Grow Rich?* Someone gave it to me as a joke, but it changed my life. Being rich took on a whole new meaning for me. It went far beyond the accumulation of money and material possessions. Hill spoke of being rich in experience, relationships, and life.

Out of the many principles he presented, the one that had the strongest effect on me was his idea of a Master Mind Group. The Master Mind Group consists of two to three very special people. Some may call this a support group.

> To make a major quantum leap in your life, you must be willing to both ask for and give support. Break through the Illusion of Separateness.

This Master Mind Group not only provides support on a personal level, but also provides a collective support mechanism for successful brainstorming and other forms of idea generation.

I choose to call it a Power Group. Hill defines power as "organized and intelligently directed knowledge." In this sense, power refers to an organized effort sufficient to enable an individual to translate desire into action. He further defines the idea of such a group as "coordination of knowledge and effort, in a spirit of harmony, between two or more people, for the attainment of a definite purpose."

Therefore, the key to a Power Group lies in the people you choose. Hill said they must be in harmony with you. The people you choose must be willing to persist, explore, give and take positive criticism without assuming a defensive posture, and be willing to listen. Above all, they must trust and be trusted. These are the people you can confide in, be vulnerable with, and be committed to. It is the chemistry of the group, its synergy, that provides the source of power for a quantum leap.

A Power Group goes beyond friendship. The group will provide you with that magical synergy: $1 + 1 = 3$, the whole being greater than the sum of its parts. It is your brainpower multiplied. If you want to take the leaps that move your life to higher levels of quality, you cannot do it alone.

You may want to choose another name instead of Power Group or Master Mind Group, but whatever you call it, the power of your braintrust will serve you in your journey. Together, you can provide support for one another. The group produces its own creative explosion. You ignite one another with energy, opening doors not possible to open alone.

Q LT *CREATIVE ADVICE*

DEFINE THE PROBLEM.

> Within the problem is the solution to the problem.
>
> —Chinese proverb

Years ago a good friend sold me an ancient Oldsmobile Cutlass that had been in storage for a long time. I was attracted by its low mileage and immaculate condition. I thought it was ideal for local transportation.

First the car stalled two miles from my home; it was towed to a nearby garage where I had the points and plugs replaced. A week later I found myself stranded in the Bronx. Again the points and plugs were replaced, and I was assured the problem was taken care of. Two weeks later the car stalled in upstate New York. Then in another week I had problems on the back roads of Connecticut. This time the car backfired and the muffler blew off.

I was furious. I knew I didn't have the knowledge or the information necessary to solve the car problems myself. I called my father, who immediately told me to have the coil replaced. I did. A year and a half later the car was still running perfectly.

Until the problem was defined, I couldn't solve it. It's the same with life's problems, and very few people take the time to truly define the problems they're trying to solve. Until they do, no solution will work.

You can start defining life's problems with a few questions:

1. Where am I now? Where do I want to go?
2. What resources do I have? What resources do I need?

3. Is there more than one problem? If so, what are the sub-problems? Now ask yourself—or your group—the following two questions at least five times, listing whatever answers come up. Continue to ask the questions repeatedly until you have exhausted your answers.

  a. What do I *really* want from this situation/project/company/person/job, etc.?

  b. What is the *real* problem?

Q L T *CREATIVE ADVICE*

BRAINSTORM.

> There are two ways of spreading light: be the candle or the mirror that reflects it.
>
> —EDITH WHARTON,
> author

Brainstorming is a popular group creativity technique. It's even listed in *Webster's New World Dictionary* as "the unrestrained offering of ideas or suggestions by all members of a group meeting, as in a business planning conference." The term itself suggests using the brain to storm a problem. The process extends the intelligence by including imagination, intuition, and inspiration.

This technique was popularized as early as 1938. However, the concept was not entirely new even then. A similar procedure had been practiced by Hindu teachers for more than four hundred years.

I have found brainstorming to be the easiest, fastest, most efficient, and most enjoyable way to achieve a quantum leap. It's deceptively simple. A group of people get together to toss ideas around. They choose a leader, who has two functions: to encourage the greatest quantity of ideas possible and to make sure that judgment is suspended during the all-important first phase. Gathering inspiration and energy from one another, they build on one another's ideas until enough information is assembled to make a list.

Then the second critical phase takes place. Choices are

analyzed and broken down to a manageable few, culling out the unworkable, leaving only the best.

Supreme Court Justice Oliver Wendell Holmes once remarked, "Many ideas grow better when transplanted into a mind other than the one where they sprang up."

Brainstorming involves three key elements:

1. The People.

I strongly suggest that the group consist of people with varying skills and different backgrounds, a heterogeneous mix. For example, a brainstorming session in a corporation could consist of heads of separate departments, such as marketing, sales, R&D, and management. If possible, include someone from outside the company altogether, such as a lawyer, a creative consultant, even a musician or a writer. The more diverse the group, the greater the chance for the perfect idea.

2. The Place.

The physical space must be comfortable and free of distractions, a safe atmosphere with no interruptions. If the concentration of the group is broken, it will take precious time to regain the original focus. The space must contain the necessary equipment: corkboard, paper, tacks, and pencils.

3. The Storyboard.

Storyboarding is the presentation of ideas so that all the concepts can be seen at once. The walls of my office, for example, are covered with corkboard on which I can pin up 3" × 5" index cards with ideas about whatever project I'm working on at the moment. Sometimes there are hundreds of them—color-coded and strategically placed. By glancing at one of my walls, I can continue refining and building on ideas from previous brainstorming sessions.

You will need at least three easels to hold the corkboard, packs of 3" × 5" index cards of various colors, a large quantity of pushpins, and some black felt-tipped pens. Each idea should be written on an index card and pinned to a corkboard. You can use different colors to identify various categories.

Everyone in the group can see all the ideas on the wall at once and see their relationship to one another. Each person can then take in and process the information as a whole and offer his or her perspective.

Q L T *CREATIVE ADVICE*

LOOK FOR THE SECOND RIGHT ANSWER.

What is half of 8? The obvious right answer is 4, but what's the second right answer? Cut the number in half across the middle and you have 0. Or divide the number in half lengthwise and you have 3. Or take away half of the curves and you have an S.

There is always more than one right answer.

Everyone likes to be right, and it's easy to get stuck brainstorming when someone comes up with what appears to be the solution. In the process of idea generation, you must challenge assumptions and be flexible. It's always important to respect others' ideas; it's a necessity when it comes to brainstorming.

RULES FOR QUANTUM LEAP BRAINSTORMING

> Gems are found by sifting through tons of useless rocks.
>
> —Anonymous

Personally, I hate rules, but sometimes even I have to admit they are necessary. So here they are.

During the idea-generating phase:

1. Go for Quantity.

The purpose of the first phase of a brainstorming session is to generate the largest number of ideas possible in the time available.

2. Don't Criticize.

When you pass judgment, you dampen the creative spirit. Judgment creates fear, and fear drives the creative spirit into hiding. The leader must halt any jokes or criticism, no matter how absurd the idea.

3. Freewheel.

No matter how bizarre or absurd an idea seems, express it. This is a no-holds-barred session.

4. Hitchhike.

Take a ride on someone else's idea. Inspire each other.

5. Be Playful.

Keep the atmosphere light. Studies prove that play and humor enhance the creative process, stimulate ideas, speed up problem solving, increase learning, and in general make life more interesting.

6. Take a Break.

Plan intermissions for diversionary activities. I suggest two forty-five-minute, freewheeling, idea-generating sessions. Between them and before the critical evaluation session, stop for at least an hour. Taking a break provides an incubation period to allow the ideas to settle. Encourage the group to do something playful and different. Play cards or video games. Throw darts. Take a walk.

During the evaluation phase:

1. Don't Be Cynical.

Eliminate negative thoughts. Give every idea a fighting chance.

2. Be Practical.

Eliminate unusable suggestions.

3. Play Devil's Advocate.

Take the opposite point of view to get the most out of every evaluation.

4. Focus.

Choose the most attractive ideas and study them closely.

5. Ask Questions.

Who? What? When? Where? Why?

Q L T *CREATIVE ADVICE*

FORGIVE FAILURE AND REWARD SUCCESS.

> No one can make you feel inferior without your consent.
> —ELEANOR ROOSEVELT

Children try, fail, and try again until they get things right. Their learning process revolves around failure and the quality of the feedback. Failure must not invite punishment, humiliation, or shame. A child needs to rethink what has taken place and give it another go.

Reward and celebration are part of a child's learning process, too. When you reward a child for success, he or she will base his or her future choices on what has been rewarded. When you acknowledge failure as a natural step in the learning process, you develop and support the courage to take risks. Failure transforms itself into learning. Failure is a necessary by-product of creativity.

Q L T *CREATIVE ADVICE*

CREATE CONTINUOUS CHALLENGES.

There is nothing worse than boredom. On the factory floor, it causes accidents. In relationships, it signals trouble. In the educational system, it makes students stare into space.

It takes work to create challenges. It may mean choosing to join a group, sign up for learning adventures like Outward Bound, take workshops, listen to tapes, or read books that support the energy and courage necessary to challenge yourself and others.

THINK OUTSIDE THE BOX.

Look at the drawing below.

Connect the nine dots together with four straight lines without removing your pencil or pen from the paper. Give yourself two or three minutes.

Were you able to solve the puzzle? Look on the next page. In order to solve it, you needed to go outside the box.

Although this example may be overused, its meaning becomes more valid every day. The box represents your circumstances. Your circumstances are, for the most part, only perception. They are self-imposed boundaries that have been accepted without question. Staying within the box is staying within your boundaries. In order to make a quantum leap, you may have to cross a few boundaries. You must stretch your mind to go places where, left to its own familiar, safe habits, it would never go.

If we're not diligent, we fall victim to our ingrained habits of living in a space where barriers have become justified and accepted.

During one of my speaking engagements I addressed a medical insurance group. The focus of the convention was to encourage the sales force to make up their own rules for managing their districts and come up with new strategies for selling.

Everyone was terrified. They had become comfortable with being told what to do and how to do it. They did what they were told and assumed that compliance and loyalty would guarantee job security.

But the business climate had changed, and change demands new rules. New rules demand new ways of thinking. The company no longer had the luxury of waiting for rules to filter down from above and waiting to see if they worked. Management needed input from employees, who were closer to the marketplace, suppliers, and clients. Whether they liked it or not, these employees had to change their way of thinking. They were no longer rule followers. They were rule makers. They were expected to think up new rules—to venture outside the box. In fact, management took the box away altogether.

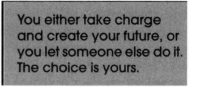

You either take charge and create your future, or you let someone else do it. The choice is yours.

We either create our circumstances or accept circumstances that have been imposed on us, like the medical insurance employees did. With a shift in thinking, we are suddenly outside the box—and that is where the possibilities are.

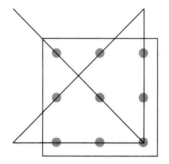

MANAGING CHANGE

Change is the law of life and those who look only to the past or the present are certain to miss the future.
—IRVING JANUS,
GroupThink

Clasp your hands together as demonstrated in the diagram below:

Now take your hands apart and clasp them back together, moving your fingers over one digit. How would you describe the difference between the two positions? Is the feeling strange, weird, unbalanced, different, uncomfortable, odd, silly, awkward, wrong?

All these words describe how we respond to change. It's no great mystery why we can want change and resist it at the same time. With a slight shift of perspective, however, change can be experienced as new, interesting, curious, or invigorating. How change is perceived is up to you.

> Every adversity carries with it the seed of an equivalent or great benefit.
> —NAPOLEON HILL,
> *Think and Grow Rich*

I've been traveling for years to the U.S. Virgin Islands to scuba dive. Upon arrival I would land on what seemed like the world's shortest runway and then walk into a giant airplane hangar, where I would be greeted by a native woman promoting Virgin Islands rum. She'd give me a small paper cup of rum punch, part of my ritual upon arrival. I would then proceed to the one and only baggage retrieval belt, where I would wait for up to half an hour to claim my suitcase. I loved that airport.

A few years ago I made a trip there after having been away from the islands for almost six months. I got off the plane and was ushered into a brand-new terminal that was air-conditioned and oddly futuristic. There were now two baggage retrieval belts. They were efficient, and even though I got my suitcase more quickly, I felt disappointed. I even lost my desire for the cup of rum punch.

I walked over to the car rental window and did my business. Because I had decided not to include the collision insurance, the attendant behind the counter had to walk me out to the parking lot to inspect the car. In transit, I asked her how she liked the new air-conditioned terminal.

She didn't appear to have heard me. I asked her again.

"I don't like it," she said curtly.

"Why?" I persisted.

"Too fancy."

I knew what she meant. Even though the change created a better environment for everyone, it was unsettling and unnatural, and she (and I) didn't like it.

There may not be much you can do about the way things change, but there is a lot you can do about how you react to it. Over that, you have total, absolute, and complete control.

> One must never lose time in vainly regretting the past nor in complaining about the changes which cause us discomfort, for change is the very essence of life.
> —ANATOLE FRANCE,
> pseudonym of Jacques Thibault,
> nineteenth-century French writer and
> Nobel prize winner

There is strange comfort in thinking that we can anticipate our future, even if the future is black. Battered women have admitted that remaining in an abusive relationship is not as frightening as leaving. People stay year after year in stultifying jobs. And I liked an old airport, even though it was small and inefficient.

But knowledge of how change works gives us the power to see all change as positive. Adapting to change is simple to talk about, difficult to execute, painful in the process, yet much less exhausting than fighting it.

> Things are more like they are now than they have ever been.
> —DWIGHT D. EISENHOWER,
> thirty-fourth president of the United States

Remember Bill Murray in the hilarious film *Groundhog Day*? What if you were in that situation? What would you do if you knew with absolute certainty that every day would be exactly like the day before? That, for the rest of your life, you would be, have, and do exactly the same as you are, have, and do now? That there would be no surprises, no spontaneity, no newness?

My bet is that, like the character in the movie, you would do everything in your power to change that. We both resist and seek change. And it's this paradox that creates behavior that is often unconscious, involuntary, and even destructive.

Life is about moving; it's about change. And when things stop doing that they're dead.

—TWYLA THARP,
dancer/choreographer

Why can't we just create and accept change as part of the natural flow of life without getting upset? Why don't we create change when we discover something in our lives that doesn't work?

The answer is twofold: loss and homeostasis.

Keep constantly in mind how many changes you yourself have witnessed already. The universe is change; life is understanding.

—MARCUS AURELIUS ANTONINUS
(Marc Antony), Roman emperor

Q L T *THEOREM*

CHANGE CREATES THE THREAT OF LOSS AND THE THREAT OF LOSS CREATES RESISTANCE.

The truth about change is that, positive or negative, it creates loss. All change involves giving up something. We fear loss and resist change.

Q L T *THEOREM*

CHANGE CAN OCCUR ONLY AFTER THE PAIN OF REALIZING THAT CURRENT BEHAVIOR CAN NO LONGER BE TOLERATED.

It's tough enough to have the threat of loss challenge us, but, in addition, our bodies and our brains have a built-in penchant to stay the same. When we stray out of our familiar boundaries, that self-protecting mechanism is alerted to possible danger and brings us back to "normalcy." Our body temperature and blood sugar levels are two prime examples of this self-regulating and protective system.

However, this system goes beyond our physical bodies and

applies to psychological states and behavior modes as well. This condition of balance, equilibrium, and resistance to change is called *homeostasis,* a universal stamp of all self-regulatory systems from microscopic bacteria to the salamander, from the human being to the family, from an organization to a culture.

This self-protecting mechanism is designed to buffer us against the shock of change by encouraging us to act in familiar ways with familiar behavior from the past, even when that behavior is inappropriate.

I once heard a golfer say, after shooting under par, "I couldn't believe how well I played today. It wasn't like me at all." The next day he played one of the worst games of his life. He balanced himself out. His homeostasis, his preprogrammed self-image, was maintained.

The feedback system in families and organizations requires a complicated form of maintenance. Reward, punishment, manipulation, instruction, approval, affection, denial of love, and rewarding with love are a few examples. Imagine the systems used by social and national cultures!

Homeostasis does not distinguish between change for the better and change for the worse. It resists *all* change.

This was painfully obvious to me when I first entered the field of clinical hypnosis. I worked with people who wanted to lose weight, stop smoking, improve their athletic performance, or change some aspect of their daily life. At first the suggestions I used seemed to have some effect, but in time most people drifted back to their old behavior. It was discouraging to them and frustrating to me.

Little did I know that these people were coping with the threat of loss. They not only encountered resistance from their families, friends, and co-workers, but also encountered resistance from within themselves.

> Keep changing. When you're through changing, you're through.
> —BRUCE BARTON,
> advertising executive, Batten, Barton,
> Durstine & Osbourne (BBDO)

In 1950 an article written by Elting E. Morison appeared in an issue of *Engineering and Science Monthly,* published by the

California Institute of Technology. Although it was a story about the development of a continuous-aim firing system for the British navy, it is tremendously valuable as a metaphor for change.

The continuous-aim firing system was first devised by an English officer in 1898 and introduced into our Navy around the turn of the century. Before that time, guns were mounted on a very unstable platform—a rolling ship. The only control a gunman had was the small gear that moved the gun up and down. Outside of that, the gunman had to wait until the roll of the ship was just right before pulling the trigger. The gun sight was of little use and it poked the gunman in the eye when the gun was fired. Obviously gunfire at sea was uncertain and ineffective.

In 1898 Sir Percy Scott, a British admiral and captain of the HMS *Scylla*, had a flash of innovation. While observing a particularly accomplished gunman take aim and fire, he came up with the idea of changing the gear ratios to accommodate the motion of the ship and rerigging the telescopes so they wouldn't move with the roll of the ship. Immediate improvements were made in the telescopic sight. A quantum leap had taken place. Naval gunnery jumped from an art to a science, and the gunman's accuracy increased about 3,000 percent in six years!

It is interesting to note that Scott did not invent the basics; he merely rearranged them in a new way, which made continuous-aim firing possible. Scott noticed possibility because he had actively been looking for it. His prepared, imaginative mind—spurred by curiosity, ready to challenge assumptions, prompted to ask questions, and nurtured by a supportive environment—gave birth to the creative process.

Scott developed his theories, put them into practice on the *Scylla*, and continued his training ideas as commander of the HMS *Terrible* in 1900. It was on a trip to China that he met up with a young American junior officer, William S. Sims. From Scott, Sims learned everything there was to know about continuous-aim firing, and he set out to educate the U.S. Navy, implementing Scott's ideas on his own ship.

You would think the change to the new technology was welcomed. Not at all. Change isn't easy, even when it's beneficial.

Over the next two years Sims submitted thirteen official reports documenting Scott's discovery. He cited records, supported the data with tests on his own ship, described the mechanisms and training procedures, and proposed modifications, but nobody wanted to listen to him.

At first he received no response, and being ignored did not make Sims happy. The tone of his letters became harsh. When he was finally answered, he was told to return to the accepted method of gunnery.

Sims was determined; he persisted. He circulated his reports to other officers in the fleet, but the bureaucracy in Washington defended the present system. When this did not shut him up, they called him an egotist and a falsifier of evidence. Undaunted, Sims took the most extraordinary step of all: He wrote to the president of the United States, his Supreme Commander.

President Theodore Roosevelt was impressed. He brought Sims back from China in 1902, designating him Inspector of Target Practice, a position Sims held for six years.

Contained within this brief history of the development of continuous-aim firing and the roles played by Scott and Sims is a model of how change and the resistance to change work.

There are three logical reasons for the immediate negative response to Sims's ideas. First, he was a junior officer, like a worker on the factory floor or a staff member at a lower management level. Second, he was three thousand miles away from the decision-making process. And third, his criticism was directed at the very men who had invented the original equipment. These reasons alone could produce strong resistance. But there is yet another, far more important reason.

Honest disbelief accounts for only a minor portion of the picture; it is the "identification paradigm" that gives resistance its power. In Sims's case, the identification paradigm rears its head twice. First, the men in charge identified with the existing mechanisms of weaponry, creating an automatic protective response. And second, those in charge felt the existing society, the Navy itself, was threatened.

When people become identified with their creation, they may become blind to new possibilities. And people who identify with a comfortable, settled way of life may devote their creative energies to trying to maintain it.

Q L T *THEOREM*

PERSONAL IDENTIFICATION WITH ANY CONCEPT, BELIEF, CONVEN-
TION, OR ATTITUDE WILL CREATE A POWERFUL BARRIER TO CHANGE.

Another interesting example of breakthrough thinking is provided by the same historian:

> In the years from 1864–1879 ten steel companies began making
> steel by the then-new Bessemer process. All but one of them at
> the outset imported from Great Britain English workmen famil-
> iar with the process. One, the Cambria Company, did not.
>
> In the first few years, those companies with British labor es-
> tablished an initial superiority. By the end of the '70s, Cambria
> had obtained a commanding lead over all their competitors. The
> Bessemer process, like any new technique, had been constantly
> improved and refined in the period from 1864–1871. The British
> laborers of Cambria's competitors, secure in their performance,
> resented all change. [Think about the old IBM.] The Pennsylva-
> nia farm boys, untrammeled by the rituals, rules, and traditions
> of their craft, happily and rapidly adapted themselves to the
> constantly changing process. . . . They ended up creating an
> unassailable competitive position in their company.
>
> —ELTING E. MORISON
> *A Case Study in Innovation*

Q L T *THEOREM*

IN ALL SOCIETIES (FAMILY, TOWN, CHURCH, INSTITUTION,
ORGANIZATION) THE NORMAL HUMAN INSTINCT IS TO PROTECT
ONESELF AND, MORE IMPORTANTLY, ONE'S WAY OF LIFE.

Whether it is the family, the Navy, IBM, or the company you
work for, there is a comfort zone of convictions, daily routines,
physical accommodations, habits, and rituals. If any of these infra-
structures is challenged, then the structure of the unit is threatened, which produces a protective instinct. This explains the resistance leveled at Junior Officer Sims.

Identification can help keep intact the nurturing aspects of family, religion, and even business, but for the most part identification limits innovation, exploration, and curiosity; it creates tunnel vision. A company exclusively identified with a specific product may not anticipate a customer's need for a new product; an individual who's identified with a specific job may not see new career possibilities.

How can the negative aspects of the "identification paradigm" be eliminated without destroying the positive benefits gained from security? Examining the saga of continuous-aim firing, we see a group dedicated to the mutual goal of national defense. On one hand, there is the limiting commitment to the status quo; and on the other, there is the equally limiting determination to change. Both sides defended and attacked, even though their goal was the same. The identification paradigm created limited perspective between the two sides, which could result only in conflict that prevented negotiation.

However, the farm boys from Pennsylvania at the Cambria Company were more interested in manufacturing steel than in holding on to an old manufacturing method. Their energy focused on a much larger vision.

Whether it's the family, the church, or a corporation, the key to managing change is purpose. Identify the purpose in the grandest terms possible, and

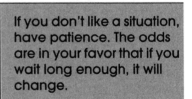

If you don't like a situation, have patience. The odds are in your favor that if you wait long enough, it will change.

you'll have created a vision. Make sure the vision is consistently communicated to every member of the group, and you'll have created solid energy. A clearly defined vision that is consistently communicated provides the fuel to blast apart the limited identification paradigm, the energy to combat resistance to change among members of any group, and the power to deal with, manage, and accept the change.

Here is what you can do to begin the education for managing change.

■ LEARN ABOUT RESISTANCE

Make a fist with either one of your hands and press the fist against the palm of your other hand. Press harder. Did you resist by pressing back against your fist with the palm of your other hand? Chances are, you did. Resistance is a natural part of the human spirit.

> To attain what we want (the desired state), we must pass through the uncertain, uncomfortable phase of the transition state.
>
> —DARYL R. CONNER,
> *Managing at the Speed of Change*

It is amazing what we will endure to avoid acknowledging pain, but in order to make quantum leaps, we must be willing to examine discomfort. Wishing it were not so is simply denying reality. Mental and emotional distress or physical discomfort may well be signals that something is out of balance or that we are caught in conflict between what we think we want and what we need. Pain must be viewed as a forecaster of possibility.

Pain is part of the process of moving from where we are to where we want to be.

Q LT *THEOREM*

IN ORDER TO CREATE CHANGE, YOU MUST BE CONSCIOUSLY AWARE THAT PAIN IS OFTEN A SIGNAL FOR CHANGE.

A man opens the front door to his home and, as he walks in, stubs his toe on a loose board. Although he thinks he really must do something about it, he takes no action. The next day he walks through the doorway and trips over the same loose board, falls, and hurts his knee. "That's it!" he vows. "I'm going to fix that board before someone really gets hurt." But he gets busy and forgets. The following day he trips, falls, and breaks his arm. He finally hires someone to repair the board.

Part of the growing process is learning to listen to ourselves. Distress is often a message that we need to make a change in our lifestyle, relationship, eating habits, job, attitude, or behavior. Pain can *activate* change. Feeling angry, sad, or agitated can be positive *if we pay attention.* Instead of resisting the distress, we can use it as a learning tool.

Awareness, in itself, is curative.

—FRITZ PERLS,
founder of Gestalt therapy

Each individual differs in tolerance. The higher the tolerance, the greater the resilience. Understanding the nature of resistance may well keep you from stumbling over your own psychic doorstep. It's scary to give up the familiar, and it's easy to underestimate the anxiety we will feel when we choose to change.

▩ CATEGORIES OF CHANGE

Change takes place in three ways.

1. Crisis Change.

Some event happens that thrusts change upon us, such as a tragedy like losing your home in a storm, a serious illness, or divorce. It could be children leaving home, retirement, unemployment, a job change, or a promotion. Our paradigm of the way things have always been is suddenly blown apart, and we see the world through a new filter.

2. Evolutionary Change.

If we wait long enough, change will occur. Unfortunately, some people even think that if they wait long enough, things will go back to the way they were.

We notice everyone else is changing and think it would be a good idea if we followed suit. The change may or may not benefit us, but what prevails is the "better late than never" attitude.

3. Visionary Change.

Visionary change is the most empowering because it is proactive. Visionary change is learning, anticipating, and creating.

You begin with the questions "What do I want to create?" and "What do I want my ideal future to look like?" No matter how much change takes place, the power of vision provides us with a center to which we can always return for personal and professional renewal.

> Some luck lies in not getting what you thought you wanted but getting what you have, which once you have got it you may be smart enough to see it is what you would have wanted had you known.
>
> —GARRISON KEILLOR,
> radio show host and author

▓ THE STAGES OF CHANGE

The process of change has three distinct stages, and the more you know about the nature of change, the easier it is to move through them.

1. Letting Go.

Resistance is at its peak: denial, despair, anger, blame, sickness, sadness, and mourning. It is in the first stage that something is lost.

2. The Dead Zone.

This is a time of reorientation. Often we feel at our worst. We feel a combination of hope and despair, confusion and adjustment. We begin searching for meaning.

> Every change looks like a failure in the middle.
>
> —ROSABETH M. KANTER,
> *The Change Masters*

3. The Leap.

In the third stage, we begin to identify with the new way. We may feel a combination of fear and excitement. In order to take the leap, we first must have let go, released the old, and fully experienced the dead zone. Now there can be creativity and comfort.

I experienced the three stages of change when I decided to move from New Jersey to Connecticut. The initial decision was agony. For ten years I had been conveniently located between two major airports, which meant I could get to either of them in less than forty-five minutes. In my business this is a real benefit. After the move I would have to allow perhaps twice that amount of time. I would be leaving my neighbors and friends. I wouldn't be able to eat breakfast at my favorite diner or work out at my local health club.

I moved, but I would drive more than an hour back to my old health club to work out. I refused to become involved in my new community, and I even paid rent on my old, empty apartment for six months. I refused to let go, and I was depressed. This was the first stage of change: denial and resistance.

I finally gave up my apartment in New Jersey, but had not yet become grounded in Connecticut. I was confused and rootless. I was experiencing a total reorientation.

Quite suddenly one day I took the leap and magic happened. I connected with others in my new community. I joined a group of professional actors and with them founded a theatrical workshop. I made friends with people at a new diner and joined a local health club. I was, once again, both creative and excited about my future. In retrospect I am surprised at how long the adjustment period took.

Once you understand the mechanism of resistance and the three stages of change, you are ready to take positive steps to handle change. You will soon recognize that, even when you feel as though you are being forced into doing something, you still have control. You have the choice to let go and accept, or resist; and you have control over your perception of how the change will affect you by consciously creating and reinforcing your picture of a positive future.

QLT *THEOREM*

MAJOR CHANGE OCCURS WHEN EXPECTATIONS ABOUT SIGNIFICANT EVENTS, ISSUES, OR SITUATIONS ARE DISRUPTED; WHEN PEOPLE EXPECT OR ANTICIPATE ONE THING IS GOING TO TAKE PLACE AND SOMETHING DRASTICALLY DIFFERENT OCCURS.

If you have always done it that way, it is probably wrong.

—CHARLES KETTERING,
inventor of the electric starter for automobiles
and founder of the Sloan-Kettering Foundation

ACTION STEPS TO MANAGE CHANGE

There are thirteen steps to managing change:

1. Be Aware.

First, pay close attention to what's going on around you. When you change or attempt to create change, you will inevitably encounter resistance. Even those who love you may unconsciously undermine you.

I knew a husband who wanted his wife to lose weight, but as she became slim, he unconsciously sabotaged her progress. As his wife's self-esteem improved and her behavior changed, he felt threatened. He hadn't anticipated that her changes would affect the entire structure of their relationship.

People often prefer to stay with the familiar and comfortable even at the expense of happiness.

Second, be aware of yourself, your work routines, your patterns of behavior, and your modus operandi. Notice if you're out of step. Think of a musical metronome. If your environment changes and speeds up the metronome, you need to move faster.

2. Be Gentle With Yourself.

You must be willing to take one step back for every two steps forward. You want long-term change, not a series of quick fixes.

Learn to recognize the warning signs of stress and keep pushing forward gently. It takes commitment, resilience, and persistence. All meaningful long-term change takes time.

3. Weigh the Pros and Cons.

If the pros outweigh the cons, if the positive overshadows the negative, give change the green light.

4. Break Down the Change Into Small Steps.

When you look at a mountain, it appears formidable. You may become overwhelmed by the thought of the amount of energy required to climb to the top. But the long, hard climb is only a series of baby steps.

Break down the desired change into small parts, each with a specific written statement and deadline date. What doesn't get measured doesn't get done. Always start with the easiest part of the change to encourage further success. You do not want to let your mind play tricks by setting up a barrier of impossibility. Once you take that first successful step to action, you're on your way.

5. Become an Orchestrator of Reality.

> Future shock is the shattering stress and disorientation that we induce in individuals by subjecting them to too much change in too short a time.
>
> —ALVIN TOFFLER,
> *Future Shock*

Since we will always move away from what creates the most pain to what creates the least, the question becomes "How much pain are you willing to endure before you decide to make a change?"

Daryl Conner points out in *Managing at the Speed of Change* that a change agent must "orchestrate pain." To be successful, you must do just that: become an orchestrator. The status quo is a powerful motivational force. You need to provide another motivation to pull others away from their present methods of operation and develop new commitments. This requires managing information in a way that creates a perceptual change.

Most people say, "I'll believe it when I see it." The truth is we see it when we believe it. Our ability to manage information directly impacts perception. Given the right information, the desired perceptions emerge from a new belief system.

What you believe is your mental pain endurance threshold is not necessarily anyone else's. To become a Quantum Leap Thinker, you must become adept at managing others' perceptions.

Q L T *THEOREM*

YOUR FRAME OF REFERENCE DETERMINES HOW MUCH PAIN YOU
ARE WILLING TO ENDURE BEFORE YOU MAKE THE CHOICE TO MOVE
FROM YOUR PRESENT UNDESIRED STATE TO A NEW DESIRED STATE.

The first step to managing perception is to accept and recognize
the distinction between your world and the world of those around
you. Everyone has a personal frame of reference through which
he or she experiences fears, desires, aspirations, and hopes. You
must challenge your assumptions. You must see the world through
the eyes of others. You must honor others' fears regardless of
your own judgment.

Q L T *THEOREM*

A PERSON'S FRAME OF REFERENCE IS A KEY UNCONSCIOUS FACTOR
IN MOTIVATING THAT PERSON TO A NEW LEVEL OF BEING.

You certainly don't have to agree with another person's point of
view to demonstrate compassion. My feelings are as valid and real
to me as yours are to you. How sad are the meager and self-
righteous attempts to dismiss or ignore other people's fears and
concerns. Jokes, impatience, or patronizing remarks never work.
Such insensitive behavior will always come back to haunt anyone
who insists on operating as if his or her reality is the only reality.

Three years ago I made a number of presentations on the
change process to organizations in the computer industry. They
knew they had to change their focus from product to service. The
health care industry came next, followed by banking institutions.
Each of these industries had its own frame of reference about the
need to change. Each held on to its resistance until the pain became overwhelming: Their businesses suffered. Imagine the individual frames of reference within these multilevel organizations
and each worker's fears, concerns, and resistance.

There are specific actions that lessen the pain of change and
foster resilience:

- Develop a critical mass of information.
- Let others know that abandoning the status quo does not mean losing control.
- Understand how much pain others can endure.
- Develop systems in which people can exercise some degree of control over what takes place in the change process.
- Create tension to motivate others.
- Be aware that each person's frame of reference is different and demonstrate with integrity an understanding of the individual's concerns and fears.
- Present changes in a way that takes into account various frames of reference.

6. Make a Contract With Yourself.

Write a contract stating exactly what change you intend to make and set a deadline for yourself. By entering into a written contract with yourself, you become your own coach.

7. Create a Routine.

Nothing worthwhile can be developed without consistent practice. Set a routine and stick to it, no matter what. Every obstacle you can anticipate, and more, will suddenly pop up: "There's not enough time." "There's not enough money." "I'd be taking time away from my family (or business)." "It hurts too much." "It's too uncomfortable." "It's not worth it." "I really didn't want to do it anyway."

It's so tempting to take a shortcut rather than learn a new skill, develop a new product, or build a healthy relationship. But every highly successful individual I have ever met has achieved his or her position by practice and commitment to a constant, consistent routine.

Pretend. Act as if the new behavior were already real. See it. Breathe it. Sense it. Feel it. In *Mother Night*, Kurt Vonnegut said to be careful who you pretend to be; you just may become that person.

8. Be Patient.

Have patience with all things, but chiefly have patience with yourself. Do not lose courage in considering your own imperfections but instantly set about remedying them—every day begin the task anew.

—ST. FRANCIS DE SALES
sixteenth-century spiritual teacher and
author, *Introduction to the Devout Life*

It takes at least thirty days to etch a new groove into your pattern. Patience is the choice of winners.

9. See the Whole Picture.

Any change within a system affects the system as a whole. When you can see the whole picture, your ability to support others increases.

10. Develop a Support System.

Support gives you the space to express discomfort and pain. Support provides a changeless center of stability and safety.

The totally independent person is cut off, physically or emotionally, from others. An overdependent person clings to situations or relationships that are often destructive. An interdependent person is willing to both give and ask for support. This creates the foundation of partnership, a base of operations from which we manage change.

11. Provide a Creative Environment and Encourage Creativity.

The tempo of ever-increasing change demands a consistent flow of new ideas. Quantum Leap Thinkers must ensure a supportive environment and set up a reward system for creative output.

12. Encourage Superb Communication Skills.

Make a point of communicating daily. Touch base consistently. When people know you're there for them, change is less difficult.

Bring the family together for meetings or, at the very least, have dinner together. At work, hold team meetings; take your department out to lunch at unexpected times. Support must be *visible* for change to take hold.

Encourage dissent. Allow people to voice resistance. When resistance is diverted, it too often becomes covert and destructive.

Acknowledge contribution. People need to be acknowledged for making a contribution, no matter how small. A small thank-you carries a lot of power to support commitment and encourage motivation.

Change your paradigm about the concept of criticism: Failure doesn't exist—only learning. Make all feedback positive and empowering. No one is his or her job, marriage, grades, golf score, or sales quota. Always separate the person from the task. People are uniquely individual, full of possibility and potential. Let the individual know that he or she is valued, wanted, needed, and appreciated.

Listen. Listen. Listen. You cannot understand simply by observing. Ask questions, listen, and empathize. People seldom want to be cheered up; they want to be heard, to be understood. Paraphrase what the other person says, so he or she knows you heard every word. Allow people to release pent-up, fear-based emotions and you will make them feel appreciated, valued, and understood. Avoid asking, "How do you feel?" unless you intend to listen to the response. Otherwise, your communication is manipulative. When you listen, you send the message that you care. What better support can you give?

13. Celebrate.

Have a party or go to a movie. Buy yourself a present or take yourself out for a great meal. Applaud your co-workers; give them a plaque or an incentive lunch. Whatever the choice, a pat on the back reaffirms personal worth. Celebration is completion. Celebration is validation.

> Faced with the choice between changing one's mind and proving that there is no need to do so, almost everybody gets busy on the proof.
> —Anonymous

Not long ago I discovered that my father is not my biological father: He adopted me. No one had ever told me. My mother was afraid that the knowledge of her first marriage and my subsequent adoption might have a negative influence on my relationship with Dave, my brother by her second marriage. To avoid conflict, she swore the entire family to secrecy.

While helping my parents move out of the house in Zion, Illinois, where Dave and I grew up, my nephews—Dave's sons—were carrying a dresser down a flight of stairs. They dropped it and the drawers fell out, spilling their contents. Hidden underneath an old piece of newspaper was a marriage certificate and a photo of my mother in a wedding ceremony with another man. Mystified, the boys brought the photo to their dad.

Dave confronted our father, who explained that I was my mother's child from her first marriage and that he had adopted me when I was three years old. Dave was horrified that I had never been told.

Six weeks after my brother's amazing discovery, I was scheduled to speak to a group of real estate agents in nearby Milwaukee. My brother and father decided this was an ideal time for the revelation.

My brother and father drove the forty miles from Zion, Illinois, to meet me for dinner. As always, I was delighted to see them and catch up on family news. I had recently gone to Grand Prix race car school and was anxious to show my father photos. I gave him the pictures, but he set them aside. That was unlike him. Something was wrong.

He looked at me in an odd way and said quietly, "Son, I have something to tell you."

I froze. That sort of intimate statement was very much out of character for him. I asked if something dreadful had happened to my mother or grandfather, but he said, "They're fine. I'm afraid it's a little heavier than that."

I felt myself on the verge of panic. What could be "heavier" than death? I glanced at my brother, who was perched on the edge of his chair, looking at me intently with a strange smile on his face.

"There are skeletons in our closet," my brother said.

I felt dizzy. "Just tell me," I begged.

There was an agonizing beat of silence, and then my father said, "Son, I adopted you when you were three years old."

I quickly glanced from my father to my brother and back to my father. They both just stared at me. It was eerie. I felt my world of reality slipping away. I was speechless.

My first feeling was a whisper of anger and resentment. My mind began to demand denial when, suddenly, another thought literally popped into my mind. *This really could be interesting.*

Then my negative side tugged me back. *This is wrong. I should have been told before.* My mind flipped back to excitement again. I wondered what sort of man my real father was. Back and forth. Back and forth. My mind-chatter went on for what seemed like an eternity, then I made a conscious decision. I recall it as clearly as the sound of a bell ringing. *I am afraid, and this is fascinating.* I still felt disoriented, but I also felt excited. Everything had changed, and nothing had changed.

In retrospect, I am very clear as to why I was able to choose the more positive attitude. I have always had total support and unconditional love from my family. That enabled me to experience the fear yet look at the possibilities. Fear transformed itself into curiosity. I saw clearly that my father had chosen me, not betrayed me.

The lesson is very simple. No matter what life presents you, you have two choices about how you respond. Resist, deny, and blame, or experience the fear and look for all the possibilities that change inherently offers. Choosing to experience the fear and look for the possibilities is my definition of courage.

THE FOURTEEN POINTS OF
QUANTUM LEAP THINKING

As you remember from the diagram of the Quantum Leap Thinking process in Chapter 1, balanced precariously on the triangle foundation is a rectangle of fourteen points:

These fourteen points will appear and reappear throughout the book. For discussion, they can be separated. However, to make a quantum leap, they cannot. They may be in any order, but they must act together and in harmony.

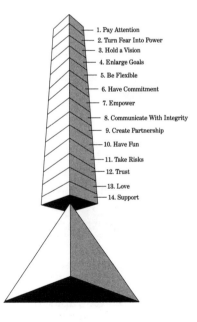

1. Pay Attention
2. Turn Fear Into Power
3. Hold a Vision
4. Enlarge Goals
5. Be Flexible
6. Have Commitment
7. Empower
8. Communicate With Integrity
9. Create Partnership
10. Have Fun
11. Take Risks
12. Trust
13. Love
14. Support

▦ THE FOURTEEN POINTS

1. Pay Attention.

Paying attention moves far beyond watching and listening. Like focusing the lens of a camera, paying attention allows us to see things more clearly and things that we might otherwise have missed. Paying attention improves communication and enhances the self-esteem of the people around you.

2. Turn Fear Into Power.

FEAR is False Evidence Appearing Real. Fear can be a message to pay attention, or it can become a barrier that keeps us from achieving what we want. How we allow fear to affect us determines our progress toward the leap.

3. Hold a Vision.

A clear vision is the driving force behind the individual, a team, or an organization. A vision that coincides with your personal values and offers a win for everyone establishes a superior level of commitment.

4. Enlarge Goals.

Goals by their very nature are limiting. To rise to the next level, you must learn to move from your current view of the situation to a better view. The skill of enlarging goals is the willingness to answer the question "Is this as big a game as I want to play?"

5. Be Flexible.

Change is far too rapid for us to have rigid rules. Whether it's on the factory floor, in the corporate office, or in the home, flexibility allows for faster course correction, less stress, and a quicker response time to others' needs.

6. Have Commitment.

Commitment propels the quantum leap, and commitment exists only when you feel a personal stake in the outcome. Commitment requires making yourself an integral part of the creation of that outcome.

7. Empower.

Empowerment gives you and those around you the training, space, freedom, authority, support, and resources to do the best job possible. Empowerment creates authority and ownership.

8. Communicate With Integrity.

You are your word. What you communicate is how you are perceived and who you are. When you take personal responsibility for your communication, you create partnerships of the highest level.

9. Create Partnership.

Partnership creates synergy, and synergy creates something larger than the power of the individuals involved. 1 + 1 becomes 3. Interdependence is the center of any relationship, whether it's family, team, community, or corporation.

10. Have Fun.

Fun is not necessarily frivolous. Fun is an attitude that creates a healthy atmosphere for learning, creativity, innovation, and productivity.

11. Take Risks.

Risk taking is the catalyst for continuous learning, innovation, and growth. Encourage risk taking in others and take risks yourself. The benefits of taking a risk almost always outweigh the results of playing it safe.

12. Trust.

Trust comes from faith. When you have done all that you can do, it is time to trust. Both self-trust and trust in others are key elements in taking the quantum leap.

13. Love.

Psychologist Gerald Jampolsky says, "Love is letting go of fear." Love is unconditional. Love is the most empowering filter we can look through because when you choose to see the world through the eyes of love, you respect the dignity of others and reduce negative stress in yourself and others.

14. Support.

Support promotes the confidence to think creatively, take risks, and deal with ambiguity. The successful Quantum Leap Thinker both asks for and gives support.

Building the foundation and balancing the fourteen building blocks is work, but you've already learned you have the tools to do it and the people to help.

LAYING THE GROUNDWORK

Paradoxical Thinking and the Power of Paradigms

The universe is made up of facts and their opposites. We are usually not aware of the paradoxical nature of things because we cannot see both sides at once. However, look at the cube below.

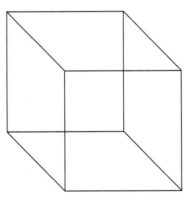

At first glance, you may be looking at the cube from above. When you shift your perspective, you see the cube from below. And with another shift of perspective, you can see the cube with one side prominent.

ONCE A CHOICE IS MADE, ALL OTHER POSSIBILITIES CEASE TO EXIST.

Regardless of intellect, education, or willpower, you cannot shift this pattern of twelve lines so you can see all points of view at once. When you choose a perspective, however, the paradox is momentarily resolved and all other other possibilities disappear.

The paradoxes of the physical universe are resolved in similar fashion. With every choice you make in the moment-to-moment existence of your life, you create your reality, and you can make the best choice when you explore all the options. But first you have to be aware of them.

Quantum Leap Thinkers are aware that there is always another side to any situation, and the opposite side is just as valid as their point of view. It's a tough concept to grasp, especially if you really believe you're right, but it is the acceptance of others' differences that jump-starts the empowerment process, ignites teams, and leads to managing diversity.

▨ THE POWER OF PARADIGMS

Thomas S. Kuhn introduced the concept of paradigms to the scientific world twenty-five years ago in *The Structure of Scientific Revolutions*. Kuhn, a scientific historian, considered paradigms a whole new way of looking at and predicting possible outcomes. He wrote that scientific paradigms are "accepted examples of actual scientific practice, examples which include law, theory, application, and instrumentation together . . . [that] provide models from which spring particular coherent traditions of scientific practice."

Joel Arthur Barker, teacher, advertising executive, corporate trainer, and author of *Future Edge: Discovering the New Rules of Success*, introduced the concept of paradigms to the corporate world with great success.

But what is a paradigm?

For our purposes, a paradigm is a set of rules, mind-sets, regulations, or procedures that create boundaries or limitations and tell you how to conduct your behavior (make your choices) within those boundaries or limitations in order to meet with success.

A paradigm is a filter through which we perceive, interpret, and understand our reality and our options. For example, if you were born with red sunglasses on, everything you see would be tinted red. But suppose you met a man wearing green sunglasses. You wouldn't know that he saw the world differently from you. Everything you see is red. Each of you would experience reality in a different color and not know it. You'd say the world is red. He'd say the world is green.

Who's right? This could lead to disagreement, arguments, or war. You would both believe you were right and, given your limited awareness, you both would be.

Whether it's Wal-Mart or IBM, the United States or South America, upon close examination you will discover each culture contains an amalgam of paradigms. We can see paradigms of how children should be raised, what values are important, or how we deal with relationships.

A paradigm is like a board game. The nature of the board, no matter the size, creates boundaries that limit the field of play. Take chess, for example. Chess has a very rigid set of rules. In order to win, you must plan a strategy, be somewhat flexible, and make the correct moves. If you go outside the rules and decide to play by the rules of checkers, jumping and eliminating the pieces, you would be disqualified.

In the mid-1970s I attended a convention with several speakers including Marilyn Ferguson, Joseph Campbell, and a wonderful, wild character by the name of Richard Bandler, who began his workshop by throwing a stool across the room and muttering some unprintable comment about genetics.

After studying the techniques of noted hypnotherapist Milton Erickson and the humanistic psychologist and teacher Jean Houston, Bandler and linguistics professor John Grinder developed a philosophy of their own called Neuro-Linguistic Programming, or NLP. Bandler and Grinder believe our behavior comes out of our programmed belief systems (components of our paradigms) and that we could learn to change any behavior we choose with the proper tools.

Bandler used maps as a metaphor for paradigms. According to Bandler, we all carry our own maps with us. They interpret how we see the world; they show us the way things are and the way things should be. The maps of the way things are provide us with our reality; the maps of the way things should be create our judgments.

Our maps are the result of events, the beliefs of our families, peer groups, teachers, religious leaders, the elements of our environments, and genetics, too. Some of these maps we can't change; some we can.

It is important to note that no map is the actual territory, but simply a representation of the territory. Alfred Korzybski reflects in *Science and Sanity,* "Important characteristics of maps should be noted. A map is not the territory it represents, but if correct, it has a similar structure to the territory, which accounts for its usefulness."

A map is never "real." And if the map is flawed, you can get lost.

Pretend you are in New York City, and you want to find a specific location in Greenwich Village. You are given a map at the Port Authority Bus Terminal and sent on your way. But try as you may, you are totally lost. You are frustrated, angry, and scared.

At first you think something must be wrong with you, that it's your fault. You remember a book you once read on positive thinking. *Try harder, persist, think positive,* and *smile.* But that doesn't work. It just makes you feel guilty, remember?

Finally you get there by asking directions and eventually discover that the mapmaker had made a mistake. All the energy you expended was wasted because of the map, not because of your lack of positive thinking, energy, resourcefulness, persistence, commitment, or intelligence.

Q LT *THEOREM*

WE SEE THE WORLD, NOT AS IT IS, BUT AS WE ARE.

We interpret our experiences through our mental maps without ever questioning their accuracy. It is natural to assume that the way we view things is not only the way they really are, but the way they should be. Our attitudes, choices, and actions grow out of these basic assumptions. We assume that our reality is the only reality.

By learning to rearrange our maps to match the way things are rather than the way we want them to be, we can eliminate a great deal of stress, but first we have to recognize that other possibilities exist.

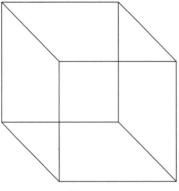

Figure 1.

Observe the paradoxical cube once again in Figure 1. Which end do you see projected outward? It depends on how you switch your perspective. You have choices.

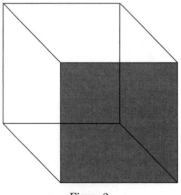

Figure 2.

But if I darken one end of the cube (see Figure 2), the shaded end is closest to you. In fact, it is very difficult to make the other end come forward. Your choices have now become limited. If I darken the opposite end of the cube (see Figure 3), once again your choice is limited. You see what *I* want you to see.

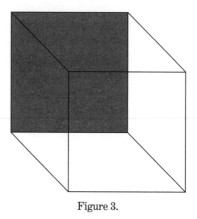

Figure 3.

Suppose you were shown Figure 2 and told that was the only way the box could be shaded. That would be your belief, your perception, your paradigm. Suppose I, on the other hand, was shown Figure 3, with the opposite end shaded, and was told *that* was the only possibility for shading the box. That configuration would become my belief, my paradigm. We meet to discuss our points of view. We might be very polite to each other, secure in the knowledge we were right in our belief, or we might get into a lively discussion or debate. Or we might argue or fight.

We all carry different points of view and perceptions. We all believe we are right. We see the world, not as it is, but as we are. For empowering communication, we must listen, share our truth, and respect the truth of others.

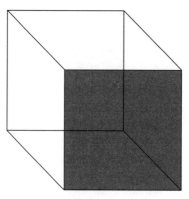

Figure 4.

Put your total concentration on the shaded box in Figure 4 for fifteen seconds. Now immediately switch your attention to the box in Figure 5.

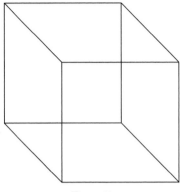

Figure 5.

Which end immediately pops out toward you? The end that will appear most prominent for a short period of time is the end you had been conditioned to see from focusing your attention on Figure 4. Even if the opposite end pops forth for the moment, the end that you were conditioned to see still ultimately dominates.

You were conditioned by looking at the box for a mere fifteen seconds. Imagine how a lifetime of conditioning determines how you view reality!

Let's take another leap in the game. Observe Figure 6. What do you see?

Figure 6.

The difference between Figure 6 and the cube is its meaning. A cube viewed from another perspective is still a cube. In Figure 6, you see either a mouse or a bald-headed man with glasses. It may take a few moments to become aware of both possibilities, but once you do, you can no longer ignore their existence, even though, once the choice is made, the other possibility disappears.

QLT *THEOREM*

ONCE A POSSIBILITY COMES INTO YOUR CONSCIOUSNESS, IT CAN NEVER COMPLETELY DISAPPEAR.

That is the power of paradigm shifting. It makes the invisible visible. To bring forth possibilities that seemed never to have existed is indeed magic.

EXPLORING TRUTH

If you would be a real seeker after truth, it is necessary that at least once in your life you doubt, as far as possible, all things.
—RENÉ DESCARTES,
seventeenth-century French philosopher

I f you believe that most of your problems are out of your control, you are voluntarily giving up your personal power and choosing to live in a comfort zone. However, consider the possibility that much of what you think is accidental is, in fact, drawn to you by how you perceive the world—your paradigms. Your thinking may be the problem.

Q LT *THEOREM*

YOUR MIND MAY NOT TELL YOU THE TRUTH, BUT YOUR BODY WILL ALWAYS TELL YOU THE TRUTH.

Do an experiment. Recall a time when you were afraid, or think about something in the future that would be terrifying to you.

You may close your eyes during the process. Concentrate on your body's reactions and notice where you feel your tension. Take a deep breath and concentrate on the physical sensations in your body.

Where did you notice tension and discomfort? In your chest? Shoulders? Face? Legs? Stomach? Now imagine another fear-based situation. The location of the tension will always be the same for you.

When you do something that goes against your personal integrity, it will cause the same reaction in your body as when you operate out of fear. Honesty and fearlessness breed balance and well-being; fear and dishonesty create uncomfortable reactions in your body, and your body sends warnings.

That physical sensation is a warning that you are doing something that is not consistent with what you believe. If you pay attention, you will hear the message loud and clear. Truth will become an internal gyroscope that will keep you and your integrity on course. Being aware of the messages your body sends you will become one of your most valuable tools for making empowered choices.

Resistance is natural, but don't always believe what your mind tells you. Get in touch with and trust your body.

■ CHALLENGE YOUR PARADIGMS

> Approach each new problem not with a view of finding what you hope will be there, but to get the truth, the realities that must be grappled with. You may not like what you find. In that case you are entitled to try to change it. But do not deceive yourself as to what you do find to be the facts of the situation.
>
> —BERNARD M. BARUCH,
> American economist

There are paradigms so commonly accepted that any chance for a change is almost impossible. These stubborn paradigms become the filter through which we see our reality.

It is natural that unseen possibilities create fear, but the unknown becomes a possibility for change. Conscious choice can only take place when you challenge what you believe to be true, your paradigms.

Q L T *THEOREM*

FEAR ONLY HOLDS POWER OVER YOU WHEN IT GOES UNACKNOWLEDGED.

As a boy I vacationed with my family in the north woods of Wisconsin. There was something wonderful about the isolation. I felt like a pioneer with limitless possibilities. We fished for many of our meals. We ventured deep into the woods and picked berries that we later sprinkled over homemade ice cream or that my mother, magically, turned into jam. Once we even caught a giant snapping turtle that, with the expert help of my grandfather, became delicious soup.

Vacations were not, however, without potential dangers. My brother and I were taught how to recognize poisonous plants, how to bait a hook without sticking the barb in our finger, and how to shoot a gun and use a knife. We were instructed how to clear an area properly to build a fire and to make sure it was out when we were finished. We were shown how to use a compass, and we were told never, ever to touch the head of a snapping turtle, even if it has been dead for twenty-four hours, unless we wanted to lose a finger.

We were taught the skills we needed to deal with the potential dangers that lurked all around us, and most importantly, to be aware of our surroundings. That same awareness holds true in avoiding any type of danger. When you have conscious awareness, you can spot what stands in the way of your paradigm shifts. After all, it's all in your mind.

> We have met the enemy and he is us.
> —POGO,
> comic strip character

Let's examine some paradigms that block personal growth. I call them illusions because they are not real.

Never think you know it all. Though others may flatter you, retain the courage to say, "I am ignorant." Never be proud.

—IVAN PAVLOV,
Russian physiologist

THE ILLUSION OF SEPARABILITY

Separability is the belief that your actions do not directly impact anyone else, that your behavior in a relationship has no effect on your partner, that your performance on a team does not directly influence the performance of the team as a whole. But the belief that you are powerless, unimportant, without influence, and that you do not make a difference is a denial of cause and effect.

As a member of a team or family, our contributions cannot be fully separated from one another; they cannot be separately measured or separately rewarded. The energy of our connectedness produces collective results.

When we take a quantum leap in our thinking, we realize that our actions have direct impact on global outcomes. We discover that we do make a difference in a system that we cannot totally comprehend.

Unfortunately, what I call the "Illusion of Separability" has been supported by the educational system, the organizational structure, and even by the family unit. Most of our reward systems encourage the individual to focus on the merit of his or her own contribution rather than on how the contribution supports a successful team.

QLT *THEOREM*

TO MAKE QUANTUM LEAPS, WE MUST RESPECT THE DIGNITY OF THE INDIVIDUAL AND DEVELOP THE AWARENESS THAT WHETHER IN A FAMILY, ORGANIZATION, OR SOCIETY, WE FUNCTION AS LIVING, BREATHING SYSTEMS, EACH AFFECTING THE OTHER AND CAPABLE OF SELF-RENEWAL.

The Illusion of Separability is a block to a win/win way of thinking; it encourages the mind-set that if I win, you lose. It gives credibility to the assumption that competition is the only way to play.

Once you choose to change your thinking (shift your paradigm), you will begin to experience your connectedness with others. You will discover that people are your greatest resource, and with that discovery comes the motivation to treat others with respect, dignity, and appreciation.

I've had the privilege to be associated with some of the most successful individuals and organizations in the world, and one of their common denominators is a commitment to other people. Genuine caring for others directly contributed to their success.

You may be the center of your own universe; however, realizing that you are not the center of the *real* universe can be frightening. It's an awesome discovery that every time you come in contact with another individual, make a phone call, smile, frown, lose your temper, discipline, blame, love, act, or don't act, you influence someone or some situation. Whether you like it or not, you directly affect those around you.

And the people you have influenced spread your influence like the ripples created after a pebble has been thrown in a pool. Influence creating influence: cause and effect. With that sudden realization of your personal power to effect change and make a difference must come a sense of responsibility.

Q LT *THEOREM*

THE AWARENESS OF OUR CONNECTION TO EACH OTHER IS THE KEY TO CONTRIBUTION AND SERVICE.

Breaking through an illusion that has been a natural part of your thinking is not easy. The awareness of personal power often causes fear because it means accountability. But quantum leaps can't happen until you become aware of your effect on people and are willing to be responsible for your own power.

> For fragmentation is now very widespread, not only throughout
> society, but also in each individual; and this is leading to a kind
> of general confusion of the mind which creates an endless series

of problems and interferes with our clarity of perception so seriously as to prevent us from being able to solve most of them. . . .
The notion that all these fragments are separately existent is evidently an illusion, and this illusion cannot do other than lead to endless conflict and confusion.

—DAVID BOHM,
American physicist

THE ILLUSION OF FAILURE

Failure is the one fear that always puts the brakes on creativity, innovation, risk taking, growth, and productivity, yet most of us have been programmed from our earliest years to be afraid of failure. The person who has learned not to be afraid, who has shifted his or her paradigm about failure, creates the feedback necessary for learning. He or she turns the fear of failure into personal power.

Life is an error-making and error-correcting process.

—JONAS SALK,
developer of the polio vaccine

Feedback from failure gives us the information necessary for course correction. A heat-seeking missile is off-target most of the time. An airplane is off-course the majority of its flight pattern. It is the built-in course correction system that guides the missile to its target or the airplane to its destination.

I was fortunate to have a family who constantly supported me to explore new areas. Because I was praised for my efforts and not punished if the result didn't appear to be successful, I was not conditioned to label my efforts as failure. I was taught that if others did, that was *their* problem. I was encouraged to look at any outcome, positive or negative, as a learning experience and use it as a guide in my next project.

Occasionally, of course, I was discouraged. I still am. American engineer and futurist Buckminster Fuller wrote, "Whatever humans have learned had to be learned as a consequence only of trial and error experience. Humans have learned through mistakes."

Think of three events in your life that you or someone else labeled as failure and ask yourself what you learned from them.

You will see quite clearly that there was always growth. Sometimes we learn from our own mistakes, and sometimes we learn from the mistakes of others, but learning makes life exciting, passionate, and fun.

There is no learning without risk, and there is no risk taking without the possibility of failure. Once our attitude shifts from punishing failure to rewarding risk, growth will take place in magical leaps.

◼ THE ILLUSION OF CONSCIOUSNESS

Am I a man dreaming I'm a butterfly, or a butterfly dreaming that I am a man?

—LAO-TZU,
Chinese philosopher

It is a natural assumption that the choices we make are guided by some external force or are conscious acts of will. However, there are powerful, unconscious forces within us at work. I studied these forces for years in my work as a clinical hypnotist.

The hypnotic state is rated on a scale of 1 to 6, the sixth stage being the deepest. One out of every five people is considered a sixth-stage subject. Given the right subject, a good hypnotist can implant a temporary belief system in the subject's subconscious. This suggestion is governed neither by the subject's conscious desire nor by his or her power of will. This new reality is the result of subconscious programming; yet because of what I call the "Illusion of Consciousness," the subject will believe that his or her conscious desire should win out.

For example, I can place a man in a hypnotic state, in which he appears fully awake and aware of his surroundings. Then I throw several $100 bills on the floor and tell him that he may keep them if he can pick them up. However, when he reaches out to touch the money, I tell him that each bill weighs 2,000 pounds.

The result is dramatic and instantaneous: He cannot pick up the money. He's confused. In his paradigm of what's possible, it doesn't make sense. I ask the man if he really wants the money, if he's *motivated* to pick it up. Of course he says yes, so I add more money to the pile. He tries harder, straining to the point where I must stop him.

In more than twenty years I have never lost a dime.

The second example is even more dramatic. While a subject is in a heightened state of suggestibility, I tell her she will be unable to remember a particular number. "You cannot remember the number eight," I tell her. "You cannot hear the number eight or see the number eight. For you, the number eight does not exist."

Then I ask her to open her eyes; she is fully awake and conscious.

I offer a reward to anyone in the audience who can get her to say, see, or hear the number eight. I initiate the process by having her count to ten. Naturally, she skips eight.

I encourage the audience to shout out the number, but she does not respond, because the sounds she hears make no sense to her. I write the number on a flip chart. Twenty-five percent of the time, she will see absolutely nothing. The number is invisible to her. Seventy-five percent of the time, she will see the drawn lines, but won't know what they mean.

This is not magic. The practice of hypnosis was accepted as a science by the American Medical Association in 1958, and doctors all over the world use hypnosis in their work.

And a hypnotic state is not mysterious. You actually enter and exit this state of mind many times during an ordinary day. It may happen when you listen to music, watch television, read a book, drive to work, or simply drift into a daydream. Something triggers this state. With discipline, you can learn to trigger it on your own. You can hypnotize yourself and control stress, lose weight, open up your creativity, or improve your golf game.

Hypnosis opens a channel to the subconscious, that part of the mind wherein resides our belief systems. When the hypnotist guides a person into a state where conscious judgment is set aside, suggestions can be momentarily or permanently programmed into the subconscious; then these suggestions become the individual's reality for the time being.

As with all unconscious programming, our senses are manipulated to perform in harmony with our beliefs, our paradigms. The output (behavior) is the result of the input (suggestions).

The point of the demonstrations is to show how our belief systems dictate reality. Like the hypnotized woman, you cannot and do not recognize what you don't believe to be true.

The perceptions you hold about yourself and the world comprise the core of your programming. They are usually unconscious and unexamined, yet every action you take and every decision you make is influenced by them. Your willingness to examine your unconscious gives you the power to change how you think, and thereby change your reality: man to mouse, convex to concave, victim to creator.

The possibilities are endless if you realize you yourself can create new belief systems within your subconscious, and these new beliefs can allow you to see what you didn't believe to be true. You can make the invisible visible.

How does that make you feel? Does it scare you and make you defensive? Or does it make you feel challenged and excited about opportunity?

The Illusions of Separability, Failure, and Consciousness are giant stumbling blocks. But when you explore the possibility of being connected to others, transform failure into feedback and learning, turn judgment into curiosity, and become aware of the power of the subconscious, you open the pathway to personal mastery.

> When the will and the imagination are in conflict, the imagination invariably wins the day.
>
> —EMILE COUÉ,
> French psychotherapist

8

Goals: The Pathway to Vision

We need objectives. We need focus and direction. Most of all, we need the sense of accomplishment that comes from achieving what we set out to do. . . . It's important to make plans, even if we decide to change them, so that at least for the moment we know where we're going and we can have a sense of progress. In the long run, it's frustrating, not liberating, to be like the airplane pilot who radios, "I have good news and bad news. The good news is that I'm making excellent time. The bad news is that I'm lost!" Or putting it another way, a sailor without a destination cannot hope for a favorable wind.

—LEON TEC, M.D.,
child psychologist

1. Goals Are Absolutely Necessary and Absolutely Limiting.

Good goals make use of your strengths and resources. I call these "stretch goals." Unfortunately most of us limit ourselves without knowing it. The goals we set are easily achieved, short-term maintenance goals. Or we set unrealistic goals. The illusion of accomplishment and forward movement is created, but we are not going anywhere.

Without clearly declared stretch goals and a plan of action to achieve them, you will most likely spend your life wondering why others seem to get what they want while you settle for mediocrity. Learning a strategy for achieving goals gives you the opportunity to become proactive, but only you can ignite the energy necessary for leaping to a new level.

We are built to perform. When our goal-striving mechanism is not put to its fullest use, it rusts like the parts of an old car, and we go through life functioning at minimum capacity.

Unless you consciously set goals that stretch you, your inner mechanism locks on to whatever it can. You might trundle after someone else's goal or float through life achieving a series of meaningless maintenance goals, "busy-ness without purpose." You are reduced to cleaning the house when it doesn't need cleaning, organizing and reorganizing closets, or tinkering with the car. You are not swimming forward; you are merely treading water.

Maintenance goals are necessary, but if they aren't making you stretch, they have little value. We often become consumed with short-term goals and bottom-line, quick results. We develop tunnel vision. We can't see the possibilities because, for us, they do not exist.

Goal setting is not the problem. Goals give us something to aim for and provide us with feedback and opportunities for course correction. Goals are a way of measuring, a way of keeping score. But they contain their own built-in blinders.

The moment we set a goal we put a ceiling on our possibilities. Goals come from the head; vision comes from the heart. Goals must be vision-driven.

Try a simple experiment. Think of a personal goal. Now ask yourself how you could make it bigger and more exciting. Imagine what you could add, how you could pump it up.

Whenever you set a goal, you have the choice to make it bigger. You have the opportunity to make it a stretch goal merely by thinking bigger.

Consider this story.

> A young man is learning the strategy of visualization. He imagines driving a Corvette. He pictures himself behind the wheel.

He feels the power as he accelerates. He hangs a picture of a Corvette above his desk and carries another in his wallet.

A close friend, knowledgeable about visualization and stretch-goal thinking, sees how his friend is approaching his process. Pulling his friend aside, he states, "You're thinking pretty small, aren't you?"

Our young man is stunned. "What do you mean? I'm visualizing my goal in great detail and supporting it with visual reminders. What else can I do?"

"Let me ask you a question," says his friend. "Do you have a relationship that's important to you?"

"No," our young man replies. "But I hope to someday."

"Well," responds the friend, "why don't you visualize the perfect woman sitting beside you in your Corvette?"

"That's a great idea!" So our young man creates a mental picture to include the ideal woman.

Time goes by, and the friend asks again how the young man's mental exercise is going.

"Great," says the young man. "I feel myself driving my car and I see the woman with all the qualities I desire sitting next to me."

His friend, relentless in the pursuit of excellence, tells him, "You're still thinking pretty small, aren't you?"

"What are you talking about? I'm visualizing the perfect woman sitting beside me in the perfect car. What more can I have?"

"A lot," his friend advises wisely. "Why don't you visualize the perfect woman sitting beside you in the perfect car parked in front of your ideal house?"

"Oh, come on," our man counters. "You know I can't afford the house."

2. Goals Are Never the End Result.

Goals are always steps to something larger. When you view a goal as the result, you have forgotten the process. You are on a much larger journey.

3. Goals Have a Built-in Possibility of Failure.

Q L T *THEOREM*

THE DIRECTION IN WHICH YOU ARE HEADING IS MORE IMPORTANT THAN THE ACHIEVEMENT OF THE INDIVIDUAL RESULTS.

When you fail to achieve a goal, your resolve will be tested, and you'll discover whether you are truly committed to it or if you have been deluding yourself. You may even discover that you have set a goal out of fear or the expectations of others.

4. Goals Must Be Realistic.

Your goals must be achievable. If you set goals that are unrealistic, you will become discouraged. Remember, goals are the baby steps to get you up the mountain.

5. Goals Must Be Explicit.

Vague hope does not get results. A goal must be quantitative and measurable, and it must have a deadline or time frame. By expressing a goal with a time frame, you make a commitment that can be measured.

6. Goals Must Be Written Down.

Writing down your goals crystallizes your thinking. Writing helps you create a clear and vivid picture of what you want.

7. Read Your Goals Three Times Every Day.

Carry a copy of your goals with you. Post them where they will be visible or write about them daily in your journal. It's easy to get distracted, and you will need to remind yourself to create positive actions on a constant basis. Commit to rereading your goals at least three times a day.

8. Goals Must Remain Flexible.

Goals are not expectations. Expectations create anxiety if they are not met. If you don't achieve a goal, you either set a new goal or set a new deadline. If you're headed in the right direction, you can always change tracks.

9. You Must Have More Than One Goal.

Keep a number of balls in the air. If you have a number of goals set in place, once one is achieved, you can immediately focus on the next one. There won't be that feeling of emptiness: "Is that all there is?"

Set priorities. Set lifetime goals, five-year goals, and one-year goals. Ask yourself what you might be able to do now that you might not in the future. For example, I want to go trekking in the Himalayas. I have bad knees. At seventy I might not be able to hike up mountains. So I move this goal up on my priority list.

When you think about making your dreams come true, you may not consider time as an element, but goals are just dreams with deadlines. You may have more dreams than there is time to fulfill them, unconsciously creating a classic goal conflict.

Setting your goal priorities is extremely important. But the reason behind your goals is what creates the energy to move to action. If you feel your passion is not great enough, review your goals and choose another about which you feel more strongly.

10. Mentally Rehearse Your Goals As If You Have Already Achieved Them.

The realization of your goals depends on the conditioning of your nervous system *in advance.* You notice what you have conditioned yourself to see. You will need to visualize your goals with all the vivid positive emotions you can summon up.

11. Create an Action Plan.

> If you really want to live, you'd better start at once to try. If you don't, it really doesn't matter, but you'd better start—or die.
>
> —W. H. AUDEN, poet

Outline what you need to do. It's easier to take action when you know what you're supposed to do. A plan of action creates direction and confidence.

12. Take Action Every Day.

Build momentum. The action doesn't have to be monumental. Write a letter, read a magazine article, listen to a tape, or make a phone call. The most important point to remember is never let a day go by without taking some form of action, large or small, toward achieving your goal.

Goals without action are like flowers without bees: They can't thrive. Action plans begin with exciting, emotionally charged visions. Make the following your personal goal workshop and answer the questions. Write them down in your journal or notebook.

a. Select one specific goal you would like to see actualized in five years. Make sure your goal is exciting and realistic. Don't worry about how you're going to do it; just write down exactly what your goal will look like five years from now.
b. What does that goal look like today?
One month from now?
What do you consider to be your biggest barrier?
What is your first step? (Something you can do today.)
c. What will you do each day to achieve your goal? Write down specific actions, quantities, and times. Clearly see yourself doing the task before you write it down.

▉ YOUR RETICULAR ACTIVATING SYSTEM

You have a screening device in your brain known as the reticular activating system, or RAS. Your RAS determines what you pay attention to. Your conscious mind can pay attention only to a limited amount of the stimuli with which you are constantly bombarded. To keep your sanity, you must filter out the majority of the incoming information. Your RAS determines what's important and what's superficial, but it allows you to focus only on what you *believe* is important. You will read this book and remember only the information that *you believe* is valuable; your RAS will screen out the rest.

Your RAS is neither good nor bad. It simply allows the information that supports what you believe. In short, *you see what you believe.*

QLT *THEOREM*

WHAT YOU BELIEVE DETERMINES WHAT YOU PAY ATTENTION TO.

If you could train your mind to notice what supports your goals, you would be attracted to the resources necessary to attain your desires. And if you could train your mind to break the limitations of your own goal setting, you would make quantum leaps.

▓ CURRENT VIEW VERSUS BETTER VIEW

Let's call your point of view your current view of the situation, or your CVS. You have a current view of your relationships, your job, a creative project, potential travels, or your financial situation. The current view of the situation is simply how, at this very moment, you define specific goals or expectations, and your CVS is controlled *totally* by your perceptions.

QLT *THEOREM*

YOUR CURRENT VIEW OF ANY SITUATION IS NOT SET IN STONE.

You create your CVS, and because you create it, you can create something different, something better. You can take any CVS and alter it into a better one.

For example, I had to go to Hong Kong to speak to an Australian insurance company. It had been a particularly busy season, and I was feeling a little ragged around the edges. My CVS was an exhausting plane trip, followed by jet lag, doing my lecture, stumbling back to the hotel, and taking another long flight home.

That was my CVS, but I had a choice to create a far better view of the situation (BVS). I reminded myself that the plane trip would give me an opportunity to read a new Michael Crichton novel. First class on Singapore Airlines meant excellent service, good food, and comfortable seats. The hotel where I was staying was wonderful. The client had scheduled an extra day for either relaxing or sightseeing. From that perspective, it actually sounded quite exciting. And I was getting paid to do what I love.

I created a BVS from a CVS, and as I did, I felt my mood change.

You can do that, too. Change your current view of the situation to a better view of the situation, but you need to remind yourself to consciously switch your perception.

If you practiced a martial art every day, the skill would become etched on your subconscious, and when you needed to defend yourself, you would respond as a reflex. If you repeat something to yourself one hundred times, three times a day, you will remember it when the need arises.

So repeat to yourself one hundred times, three times daily, "Change my current view of the situation to a better view of the situation."

I can make it even easier: *CVS to BVS.*

You can repeat "CVS to BVS" one hundred times in less than two minutes. Do you think you can handle doing that three times a day? Are you willing to invest six minutes out of your day to master a skill that can help you explode from mediocrity to extraordinary?

Give it a go for seven days. You will notice yourself becoming more aware of your choices. If you do this, I guarantee you that whenever you need to change your viewpoint, it will happen automatically.

In quantum physics, jumps take place in a random and unexpected fashion by a heating-up process. In life, leaps happen in the same way. When you are committed to continuous action and consistent growth, the magic will happen at the most unexpected times.

VISION: THE CATAPULT TO YOUR FUTURE

Goals are absolutely necessary and absolutely limiting. The moment you set a goal, you have established a ceiling on what is possible. But you need goals because they are the steps toward something much more important: your vision.

THE SECRET TO THE POWER OF VISION LIES IN THE QUESTION: WHAT DO I WANT TO CREATE?

Take a rubber band and stretch it between your hands. If you release one end of the rubber band, it will snap toward the hand that is still holding it and return to its original form. The tension that was created disappears.

> Vision gives direction to your dream.

Now imagine tying one end of a hypothetical rubber band around your entire being and the other end around what you consider your ideal future. If the vision of your future is compelling, solidly in place, and keeps a tight hold on that rubber band, you will be propelled toward that future. As long as this dynamic and creative quantum tension is held in place, you will whisk past barriers, problems, and all other negative circumstances until that tension is satisfied. The tension needed to move forward is exactly what commitment to and living from a vision provide.

Vision gives you the solidity to allow change to become your friend instead of your nemesis. Based on this principle, all you have to do is create a powerful vision of where you want to go.

Robert Fritz, founder of DMA, Inc., and the Technologies for Creating Seminars, writes in his book *The Path of Least Resistance:*

> Energy always moves where it is easiest to go, along the path of least resistance. Failure to acknowledge and work with this law of nature can quickly render the leader ineffective. The fundamental structures in most organizations channel energy naturally toward maintaining the status quo. To create lasting change, leaders must learn to create new structures which redirect the system's energies toward the desired changes.

Energy always moves along the path of least resistance. So if our energy is not moving toward a compelling future, it is because something is funneling that energy in a different direction, toward the reinforcement of old patterns of behavior instead of change and growth.

Old paradigms create resistance. The very nature of our society resists change. Innovative people are often viewed with alarm, but if we consider creativity just a rearrangement of what already exists or just plain and simple problem solving, we can still operate "inside the box."

Q L T *THEOREM*

IF THERE IS TENSION, THERE MUST BE RESOLUTION.

The concept of tension/resolution can be found everywhere, from winding up a child's toy to the formation of the universe.

Some tension/resolution systems are extremely basic: If we're
hungry, we eat; if we're tired, we sleep; if we're thirsty, we drink.
Tension. Resolution.

Challenges occur when there is more than one tension/resolu-
tion system taking place within a single structure. Take, for example, the desire to lose weight.

Individuals who want to lose weight usually have the best of
intentions. They commit to changing their bodies and diligently
launch into a weight-loss program. But without knowing it, they
confront structural conflict; more than one tension/resolution system is operating within their lives.

Their resistance to change creates one tension/resolution system; their desire to lose weight creates another, working at cross
purposes. Since tension will always seek resolution, the direction
the person moves will be dictated by the amount of tension in each
tension/resolution system at a given moment.

Here's how it works: I believe I am overweight and make a
decision to lose a few pounds. I go on a diet and manage to be
successful for a while. But then I get hungry and feel sorry for
myself. Tension. When I'm hungry or feel sorry for myself, I eat.
My resolve breaks down and I eat. Resolution. I gain the weight
back that I lost, perhaps even adding on a few more pounds. I get
angry with myself. Tension. I go back on a diet. Resolution. But
once again, I break it and the pattern repeats itself. I get frustrated, angry at myself, feel hopeless, and finally I give up.

Robert Fritz believes, "The majority of individuals have a dominant belief that we are not able to fulfill our desires." Where does
such a belief come from?

We are taught limitations. These limitations, these beliefs, are
based on what our parents or teachers thought was necessary for
our survival. We were told, with great authority, why we should
or shouldn't do certain things, but unfortunately many of these
lessons were unconsciously based on fear. The intention was probably admirable and meant to guide and help us, but the end result
was a transmission of fear.

The two most common negative beliefs we learn as children are
powerlessness and unworthiness. We learn early on that we can't
control reality; we can't make happen what we want to happen.
Psychologists call this "learned helplessness." Further, we are
taught that good behavior is rewarded; bad behavior punished.

Therefore, if at first we aren't rewarded with success, we figure we probably didn't deserve it anyway.

Actors, painters, and musicians often say to be a true artist, one has to be poor. Suffering is a necessary part of the process; money imparts impurity to their art. While they struggle for recognition, they make unconscious choices to avoid money, because money does not represent freedom to them; it symbolizes something negative. The result is two rubber bands creating tension in opposing directions: One direction is the desire to be rewarded for their work; the other is to avoid all that would give them the very thing they desire.

The force of one rubber band pulls toward the vision; the other counteracts. On one side, there is a burst of energy that propels them toward their vision: resolution. On the other side, the tension of unworthiness or powerlessness increases, creating a structural conflict of tension.

We may choose to operate within a zone where these uncomfortable feelings can be tolerated, a comfort zone of tolerable conflict. The boundaries between the desired result and the feeling of powerlessness shrink, but we have created our own psychological trap.

We want to remain in our comfort zones, to play it safe. We may minimize our losses, but we also limit our aspirations. Although playing it safe makes behavior predictable and realistic, it undermines creativity and discourages risk taking.

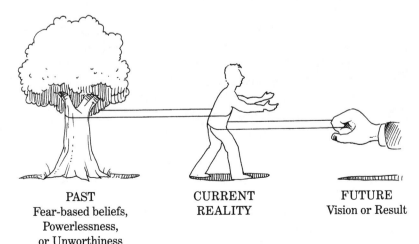

PAST	CURRENT	FUTURE
Fear-based beliefs, Powerlessness, or Unworthiness	REALITY	Vision or Result

THE RECOGNITION OF STRUCTURAL CONFLICT LEADS TO ITS RESOLUTION.

We often create artificial conflict by avoiding what we *don't* want. This is one of management's, and sometimes parents', favorite ploys. They point out what horrible thing will happen if a goal isn't achieved.

Fear gets short-term results. Fear is addictive and debilitating. We may live in fear of not having enough or that what we have will be taken away. A life of anxiety and worry is barely a life at all.

The concepts of willpower and positive thinking are a cruel joke. If the map is wrong, neither willpower nor positive thinking can help you find the territory.

The rational mind is an amazing piece of machinery, yet we often fail to resolve our own conflicts. We may manipulate them, we might *try* to work them out, or we might just give up altogether. The crux of the problem is that the fear-based beliefs remain intact. If we do not resolve the conflict, we may:

1. settle for less.
2. rationalize.
3. focus on what to avoid.
4. exercise our willpower and frustrate ourselves.

Willpower, conflict manipulation, and living in a comfort zone of tolerable conflict can get short-term results and blindfold wins. Change does take place, basic problems are sometimes solved, forward movement does occur, and some things get accomplished, but at great expense of energy. People become discouraged and bitter, because they operate from the belief that the problem lies somewhere "out there" and not within themselves.

▮ CHANGING PARADIGMS AND QUANTUM TENSION

The reason most individuals and organizations do not create major changes becomes obvious when we take into account our natural resistance, our personal homeostasis. It's no wonder that the majority of us operate only within the area of tolerable conflict. We break out of the "box," move toward the positive, and then, suddenly, snap back to the familiar, even if it's negative. Then we try again, even try harder. As the cycle is repeated, what remains invisible to us is that all movement is taking place within the same structure, the same paradigm.

Q L T *THEOREM*

TO ACHIEVE QUANTUM LEAPS, A NEW STRUCTURE MUST BE CREATED THAT HOLDS POWER OVER THE PREVIOUSLY EXISTING STRUCTURE.

An entirely new structure must be created to achieve quantum leaps, a structure that creates new tension, a new path of least resistance. Robert Fritz calls this "structural tension." I choose to call it "Quantum Tension" because the new structure allows us to make quantum leaps. We can create new realities. We become the creative force.

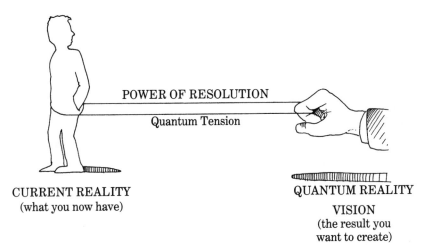

POWER OF RESOLUTION

Quantum Tension

CURRENT REALITY
(what you now have)

QUANTUM REALITY
VISION
(the result you
want to create)

The gap between what you have and what you want is the forerunner of the true creative process. Once both are clearly established, the gap between the two creates the Quantum Tension and kick-starts us into action. Tension seeks resolution.

Q LT *THEOREM*

A QUANTUM LEAP WILL TAKE PLACE ONLY WHEN YOU SEE THINGS AS THEY REALLY ARE, NOT AS YOU WISH THEM TO BE.

I used to be determined to overcome the barriers waiting to trip me up. People were constantly ignoring or disappointing me. I was often angry and disheartened. I fell into every trap that Fear, the Great Trickster, had set up.

Eventually I discovered that I was operating from a structure that could result in only one of two things: achieving what I wanted at great emotional and physical expense or achieving less than I desired. My stubbornness was a blindfold. I was held prisoner by my own belief systems, my structure.

The problem was not "out there," nor was it about what others were doing to me. The problem was my own belief system and the strategies from which I was operating. I could make only the choices available within my paradigms. I couldn't see the invisible.

The same game of discovery holds true in an organization as it does in an individual. The difficulty of the game increases exponentially with the number of people involved, but it also becomes far more interesting and powerful.

Q LT *THEOREM*

ONCE THE OPERATING STRUCTURE BECOMES IDENTIFIED, YOU HAVE THE CHOICE TO CREATE CHANGE.

Charles Dickens's book *A Christmas Carol* is the perfect example of a paradigm shift. After Scrooge is visited by the ghosts of his past, present, and future, he sees the reality of how his choices from the past have driven people away and, as a result, how he has become isolated, angry, and bitter. The ghosts reflect his self-imposed separation and mirror his self-centered choices. He sees his future as it will surely be if he continues operating from his past structure. His awakening comes with his awareness that he is not a prisoner of his past and present. He *can* change and, by changing, create a new future for himself. Scrooge makes the quantum leap, but first he had to be made painfully aware of his reality and the choices available to him.

Patrick Stewart (TV's Captain Jean-Luc Picard on "Star Trek: The Next Generation") adapted *A Christmas Carol* into a one-man Broadway show. Stewart told me that he chose the character because, like Scrooge, he underwent a major personal paradigm shift. His intense identification with Scrooge's life may be why his performance was so remarkable.

> Have the courage for great sorrows of life and patience for the small ones; and when you have laboriously accomplished your daily tasks, go to sleep in peace. God is awake.
> —VICTOR HUGO,
> French writer

Robert Fritz writes, "In willpower manipulation, it is 'See no evil.' In conflict manipulation, it is 'See nothing but evil.' In the area of tolerable conflict it is 'See neither good nor evil.' "

The majority of us will do anything rather than face reality when it is too uncomfortable. We avoid confrontations. Medical research indicates that we are partners in creating our own illnesses. We eat unhealthy food, refuse to exercise, and stay in destructive relationships, but we refuse to admit that it has any effect on our health.

The willingness to honestly view our current reality is what creates Quantum Tension. A clear view of where we are *now* promotes movement toward our vision. It is the *clarity* of our vision that empowers us.

> Without a vision, the people perish.
> —Proverbs

Without vision we lack direction; we drift about buffeted by situations, events, and people. Our lives have no joy, passion, or spirituality. It becomes increasingly difficult to crawl out of bed. We focus on finding solutions to problems at hand, but change creates chaos, and our choices are limited, because we can't see them even when they're there. We may function, but there is purpose without passion.

> If a man advances confidently in the direction of his dreams to live the life he has imagined, he will meet with a success unexpected in common hours.
> —HENRY DAVID THOREAU,
> American writer

▓ WHAT IS VISION?

A vision is about greatness. It goes beyond the individual. It may be eliminating world hunger, cleaning up the environment, re-creating our educational system, or serving others, but a vision is always about something beyond ourselves.

Vision is the beginning point for the journey, the instrument that tightly focuses all of our sights and actions on what we want to become tomorrow; it is not what we were in the past or what we are in the present. Continually focusing on a vision disciplines us to think strategically.

Vision is creating an ideal future with a grand purpose. It plays a core role in our activities, from career choices to selecting our friends, from planning family vacations to managing organizational change.

> You are not here merely to make a living. You are here in order to enable the world to live more amply, with greater vision, with a finer spirit of hope and achievement. You are here to enrich the world, and you impoverish yourself if you forget the errand.
> —WOODROW WILSON,
> twenty-eighth president of the United States

It is a common misunderstanding to equate a mission statement with a vision. The difference is vast. A mission statement comes from the head; a vision comes from the heart. A mission statement outlines what comprises our business: its goals, ranking, return on equity, net assets, increased profitability. A mission statement is a reason for being. A vision, however, cannot be expressed in numbers. A vision is a consciously created fantasy, a waking dream, yet beyond a dream. A vision is reality that has not yet come to be.

This "vision thing" is not new to the corporate world. A vision statement is often another name for guiding principles or core values. Those in a management position are slowly coming to the realization that it is their responsibility to make sure each and every employee is involved in creating the vision, and that it is the responsibility of each employee to create his or her own personal vision and incorporate it into the whole.

For example, my parents had a vision of our family vacation. It started with a destination. We all knew where we were going, but didn't know the details or side trips, and my brother and I were allowed to contribute our ideas. We took part in the creation of our vacation vision, and our participation added to the excitement of the adventure.

> We don't take the trip; the trip takes us.
> —JOHN STEINBECK,
> American novelist

There are many types of visions. We have a vision of how we want our children to grow up, where we would like to live, or what kind of job we would like to have. I call these multiple lifestyle visions "general visions." They are a necessary part of living, but general visions are not where the greatest power lies. The greatest power lies in a "Grand Vision," a vision of greatness that has six definable parts.

1. A Grand Vision Is Always About Others.

> Wealth, like happiness, is never attained when sought after directly. It always comes as a by-product of providing a useful service.
> —HENRY FORD,
> American automobile manufacturer

Challenge the short-term, quick-result "me, me, me" way of thinking. A vision of greatness focuses on service, adding value, and empowering others. The long-term success of any organization represents more than market share or profit. Long-term success makes a contribution. Greatness is what we offer one another. A vision of greatness concerns acts of service. Vision inspires commitment because it is worth pursuing for its own sake.

Tom Peters and Nancy Austin, in *A Passion for Excellence*, celebrated Stew Leonard's Dairy Store in Norwalk, Connecticut, as a terrific example of successful customer service.

If you have never heard of Stew Leonard's, you should know that calling it a dairy store is like calling an ocean a big lake. Stew's carries a purposefully limited variety of products. It has its own bakery, dairy, and butcher shop. The store is an edible Disneyland, filled with fresh fudge, popcorn, ice cream cones, singing vegetables and animals, a children's petting zoo, and many smiles. Stew Leonard's delights its customers.

In front of the Norwalk store is a six-ton rock, on which is carved the following:

OUR POLICY

Rule #1: The customer is always right!
Rule #2: If the customer is ever wrong, reread Rule #1.

—STEW LEONARD

The customer is *always* right, even when it's unreasonable and extremely inconvenient. It is that vision that empowers employees to do whatever it takes to make the customer happy, even if it might mean a short-term loss. Inherent in a true vision is long-term thinking. At Stew Leonard's, they realize that if they lose a customer, they are not just losing a $50 shopping excursion. They are losing 52 weeks times $50, or $2,600 per customer, times x number of years a customer may shop at the store.

It is easy to become so customer-focused that your employees and family members are forgotten, but Stew Leonard's constantly acknowledges its employees. There is a wall festooned with photographs of honored employees; at the cash register lines, there are television monitors playing videotapes of employees at work, waving at the camera and smiling.

Stew Leonard, Sr.'s, vision extends to include his employees. He insists that employees be treated as though they were the store's best customers. It all works.

The power of vision can overcome the greatest adversity, and Stew Leonard's is a perfect example. For years Stew Leonard, Sr., and his vision had been a shining example of great customer service, but in 1992 he was convicted of tax evasion and sent to prison. The community was devastated, and so were his customers and friends.

I assumed that the tax problems and resulting publicity would have a profound negative influence on the store's business and the attitude of the employees, so when I was asked to address its managers, I decided to speak with several employees in different departments. While they were certainly dismayed by what had taken place, every person I spoke with not only wanted to continue working at Stew Leonard's but also considered it a joy to be there.

When I addressed the employees as a group, they were receptive, energetic, inspired, and motivated. Everyone constantly communicated Stew's vision of greatness—serving others—and they all continued to act congruently with that vision.

Despite what could have destroyed many businesses, Stew Leonard's is thriving. When the vision is right, seemingly impossible odds can be overcome. The impossible becomes possible.

2. A Grand Vision Is Idealistic and Spiritual.

Our spiritual side is usually ignored except on special occasions. Day-to-day living is centered around practical matters. Yet when our spiritual nature is touched, day-to-day living takes on a different meaning.

Observe history to view the power of our spiritual nature in action. In *Man's Search for Meaning,* Viktor Frankl recounts his experiences at Auschwitz. Frankl, like millions of other innocent people, was at the mercy of ruthless, evil, arbitrary forces. Survival was beyond personal control. But for some, a responsibility for their own future empowered them to survive. Frankl was convinced that those who survived did so because they had a strong and vital spirit, a vision of their own survival. They were connected to a force greater than "self."

Martin Luther King, Jr., inspired twenty million Americans with his vision. President John F. Kennedy energized millions more to ask what they could do for their country. He empowered space explorers to take one giant step for mankind, not simply land on the moon. Mahatma Gandhi led 450 million Indians to passive resistance with his vision of independence. Lee Iacocca convinced six hundred congressional leaders and two hundred thousand automotive workers to sacrifice their time and salaries to save Chrysler Corporation.

There are uncounted numbers of unrecognized individuals in education, religion, politics, and even at home who have made a significant contribution by inspiring others with the magic of their vision. It is no accident that the business world is exploring the concept of vision and seeking ways to accomplish a higher purpose.

3. A Grand Vision Must Be Authentic.

Be so true to thyself as thou be not false to others.

—FRANCIS BACON,
English philosopher and statesman

Authenticity means that the vision comes from you, based on the integrity of who you are. It must be totally honest, and no one can make the statement for you. The vision must be recognized as uniquely yours. A Grand Vision is an extension of your being.

4. A Grand Vision Must Be Extraordinary.

Great spirits have always encountered violent opposition from mediocre minds.

—ALBERT EINSTEIN

A Grand Vision is a quantum leap from the ordinary. If it spells out your highest ideals and wishes, it will stand above the commonplace. It will be radical and outrageous. It will set you apart from the crowd. You will be criticized and misunderstood.

Historically, we have great respect for radicals with vision. Although Socrates, Gandhi and Jesus were scorned and punished, their individuality, and their vision, created greatness.

5. A Grand Vision Comes From the Heart.

> One pulse of passion-youth's first fiery glow
> Is worth the hoarded proverbs of the sage . . .
>
> —OSCAR WILDE,
> Irish writer

I have few heroes, and Dr. W. Edwards Deming is one of them. In the 1950s, after his ideas on quality management were rejected in the United States, he went to Japan, where he had a major impact. Japan's highest award for quality in business is the Deming Award. American businesses followed, adopting Deming's "Fourteen Points to Achieve Quality" as corporate guidelines.

At ninety, Deming still worked a heavy schedule. His credo was constant learning and growth. In fact, he ended his first letter to me with: "I'm sure I have a lot to learn from you." I think now that he may have answered all his correspondence that way.

The important thing is that he worked from a belief that was his and his alone. He acted from the heart.

6. A Grand Vision Is Value-Based.

Values are the foundation on which your Grand Vision is built. Values motivate, inspire, articulate, guide, and galvanize.

Crafting and communicating a vision is tough. Sustaining a vision is tougher still. But it has worked, and will work, if you are committed. As Stephen Covey, author of *The Seven Habits of Highly Effective People*, says, we must start at the beginning with the end in mind. Your Grand Vision is the fountain of greatness from which your goals flow forth. And your Grand Vision must be centered on specific values.

THE MAGIC OF VALUES

He who knows much about others may be learned, but he who understands himself is more intelligent. He who controls others may be powerful, but he who has mastered himself is mightier still.

—LAO-TZU

I have a beautiful handcrafted brass kaleidoscope that sits on the corner of my desk. It's a metal tube about ten inches long, with a lens at either end. Attached to one end is a wirelike cage in which I can place a marble.

Not just any marble: It has to be a large, semitransparent marble that, as children, we called a "boulder." Boulders come in all designs, with swirls of bright colors trapped inside. Like snowflakes, each one is unique.

When I place a marble in the wire basket and hold it up to the light, I am greeted with a symmetrical explosion of color. When I rotate the marble, I can create what appears to be a limitless flow of ever-changing patterns. But if I play with it long enough, I discover that what I thought were limitless possibilities are restricted by the design of the marble. The patterns shift and change, but only within the limitations of the colors in the marble. If I want more patterns, I have to change the marble. New marble, new colors, new designs, new possibilities. But again, within what appears to be endless variety, I will find limits.

I view the marble as a representation of our values. Values are our most uniquely individual beliefs about what is important. Values are the mental maps of the way we think things should be; they are our deepest convictions, our primary filter through which we view reality. They are the hard drive of our subconscious. Values are collective belief systems about good and bad, right and wrong. Values are a personal compass. They provide a framework for the decision-making process; without this framework, we lose confidence. We're unsure about the paths to choose.

Once you understand how values work, you will understand the true mechanism of motivation. Values determine how we respond to any and every experience in life. When our values are satisfied, we feel happy and fulfilled; when they are violated, we feel empty. If our goals and behavior are incongruent with our values, we experience inner conflict and stress. We procrastinate or overeat. We're lazy, exhausted, angry, or sick.

Imagine that the marble represents the sum of your values, and for the moment pretend that the marble cannot be replaced. You can, however, rotate the marble to form different perceptions of your reality. Values shift with life experience, like the marble rotates, but the basic color and design are set in place.

Input began at a very early age, bringing together a combination of the environment in which you were raised and the reflected values of your parents. You were told what to do and not to do, what to say and not to say, what to believe and not to believe. If you did as you were told, you were probably rewarded; if not, you were probably punished. You adjusted, blending and molding to adapt.

The media presented heroes and role models, too. For me they were Hopalong Cassidy, Roy Rogers, the Cisco Kid, and Sergeant Preston of the Yukon. Wrongs were righted. Good conquered evil. Good guys wore white hats and no one got killed. Many of my personal values as an adult reflect the values of these earlier television characters.

Understanding what you value most is essential in forming your Grand Vision.

Try not to become a man of success but rather to become a man of value.
—ALBERT EINSTEIN

Q L T *THEOREM*

UNCOVERING AND PRIORITIZING CORE VALUES PROVIDES THE PLATFORM FOR MOTIVATION.

A few years ago I was doing a presentation on empowerment for the upper management of a large telecommunications company. We were deep in discussion about resistance to the empowerment process when one of the participants piped up. "I believe in empowering our managers and most of our senior employees," he said, "but we have some secretaries and clerks who are just plain lazy. They don't care about their jobs. You can't empower people who are completely unmotivated."

They're unmotivated because they don't care about their jobs. They don't care about their jobs because they don't think they matter. What is often judged as laziness usually has nothing to do with being lazy. It is often the direct result of an employee's belief that he or she doesn't make a difference. The employee does not know how his or her job or a particular task contributes to the big picture. No amount of reengineering, down-sizing, or right-sizing will create a difference unless employees feel personally involved and unless what they value is acknowledged.

People do not go to work to fail.
—H. NORMAN SCHWARZKOPF,
retired U.S. Army general

Let's suppose that I am motivated by money. I assume that everyone is motivated by the same things I am, so I try to motivate my employees with financial incentives; or as a parent, I try to motivate my children with promises of a bigger allowance. If I don't get the results I wanted, I think they are lazy or shiftless and treat them as such, and they react by acting that way.

Or maybe I consider myself an unsuccessful manager or a bad parent. My negative attitude and resulting behavior would reinforce negative performance from my employees or children.

If you manage or communicate from your own values and assume you're playing fair, you will very likely spend a lot of time feeling frustrated, bitter, angry, and betrayed.

If you learn to recognize and support the values of others, you'll have happier and more fulfilled and committed friends, employees, associates, and family members.

People are motivated by values that may or may not coincide with yours. Take the time to discover, in a clear and precise way, your own and others' most important personal core values. Align your values and your goals to make sure they are congruent, and then reinforce and nurture your most important values (your core values), and support and nurture by whatever means necessary the highest values in others.

> Surely there comes a time when counting the cost and paying the price aren't things to think about anymore. All that matters is value—the ultimate value of what one does.
> —JAMES HILTON,
> English novelist

Your values can shift. Your highest value at the age of twenty may be less important when you're forty, and at any age you can have a false perception of what your most important values are.

When I walked through that plate-glass window, it was a wake-up call that I was out of balance. My desire to satisfy my need for achievement and recognition was in conflict with my deeper needs of family, spirituality, physical health, and vitality. The incident gave me pause to reevaluate my core values.

Don't confuse goals with values. A goal is something you intend to accomplish; a value is something you believe in. You may think there are only a few basic values, but there can be dozens, like integrity, honesty, love, freedom, and compassion. Or you might value trust, family, humility, or service to others. Others might consider self-growth, reputation, power, or adventure a core value. But there are plenty of things we consider values.

Look through the list below and choose which are most important to you, which you consider to be your core values. You may add to the list.

Peace of mind   Flexibility
Spirituality   Honor
Fame   Security
Happiness   Recognition
Wisdom   Meaningful work
Accountability   Forgiveness
Perseverance   Comfort
Diligence   Passion
Thrift   Intelligence
Intimacy   Accomplishment
Kindness   Creativity
Acceptance   Cheerfulness
Fairness   Patience
Courage

There is *always* one value that is most important—one core value that drives all the choices we make. Not knowing what that is can cause you to make some poor life choices.

For example, I have in the past assumed freedom was my most important value and made some pretty disastrous decisions based on that and made myself and the people around me very unhappy. I finally realized I was not in touch with what was most important to me. I needed to rediscover which of my values was my number-one core value.

Here are the six values I consider my own:

Love   Freedom
Contribution   Honesty
Loyalty   Integrity

To determine which of these values is my primary core value, I can use a very specific process of comparison. Here's how it works:

I select love for my first comparison. Is love more important to me than contribution? I feel love and contribution are closely linked, but I decide that love is more important than contribution, and I now use love as a primary comparison value to challenge the value of freedom.

Is love more important than freedom? That's a hard question, but I decide that it is. Is love more important than honesty? Yes. Is love more important than integrity? Yes. Is love more important than loyalty? I feel love and loyalty are closely linked, too, but I must eliminate one. I decide that love is more important than loyalty. So love is my number-one core value, the value that drives my decision making.

To put the rest of my values in order, I use the same process. Is freedom more important than loyalty? No. Now I switch, using loyalty as my next comparison value. Is loyalty more important than contribution? Yes. Is loyalty more important than honesty? Yes. Integrity? Yes. Loyalty is my number-two core value.

Following the same procedure, I go through the rest of the list. The result of my self-questioning allows me to rank my six core values in their order of importance to me:

1. Love	4. Integrity
2. Loyalty	5. Honesty
3. Contribution	6. Freedom

I had been operating under the misconception that freedom was what I valued most. I made a lot of choices based on that. No wonder I felt restless, dissatisfied, and unfulfilled.

For me, the great benefit of this exercise was to understand how I could prevent myself from setting goals that were not aligned with my values. My choices must support and honor my top three core values of love, loyalty, and contribution, in that order, if I am to feel good about myself.

Q L T *THEOREM*

BEING CONSTANTLY AWARE OF YOUR HIERARCHY OF VALUES WILL EMPOWER YOU TO SET GOALS THAT ARE CONGRUENT WITH THOSE VALUES.

Once I accepted love as my number-one core value and loyalty as number two, I was able to understand the mechanism of my personal motivation. When I feel my actions or the actions of others threaten either of those values, I move, consciously or unconsciously, away from whatever causes that threat. For example, I might not do a favor for someone because I think that it threatens my freedom. Understanding that I value love more than freedom, I can do that special favor.

I used to fear that pushing my line of tapes and books would cheapen my message. If I reframe the goal of selling product in the context of providing a needed service, I shift my motivation.

Consider this: Person A's number-one core value is freedom; Person B's is family. They fall in love, marry, and make a decision to have children. Person A makes a conscious decision to sacrifice freedom in order to raise a family, but of course says nothing.

During the rearing of the children, from time to time, Person A feels trapped and takes the frustration out on the family. The children grow up and leave home, but the damage has been done. Had each person been aware of the other's values, they might have reached a compromise.

When you take the time to ask the right questions and really listen to the answers, you can create congruency among your goals, vision, and values. When you discover the hierarchy of your values and the values of others, you have all the information you need to empower and motivate.

Consider asking the following questions to uncover the core values that motivate and create commitment: As a partner, "What do you want out of this relationship?" As a teacher, "What do you want out of your education?" As a recruiter, "Why do you want to join this organization?" As a salesperson, "What do you want out of our product?"

QLT *THEOREM*

WE WILL ALWAYS MOVE IN THE DIRECTION OF OUR NUMBER-ONE VALUE AND AWAY FROM WHAT THREATENS THAT VALUE.

What if, as a manager, you knew you could discover the key to unlock the passion and commitment of your employees? Be a value detective. Ask one employee what's important to him or her about his or her job. If the employee answers, "Money," ask another question: "What's important about money?"

Take whatever answer the person gives you and ask the same question, "What's important about . . . ?" Suddenly, and often quite magically, you'll uncover his or her values. Sooner or later, the employee will say, "Because it buys me freedom." Or security. Or the resources to buy a family home or have another child.

Q LT *THEOREM*

THE ANTIDOTE TO THE ARROGANCE OF ASSUMPTION IS ASKING THE RIGHT QUESTIONS AND MAKING THE CORRECT DISTINCTIONS.

Words can be tricky. For example, if you and I consider love to be our number-one core value, we should be in rapport. But love means different things to different people. For you, love may mean taking care of another person. For me, it may mean being taken care of. For someone else, love may mean being physically touched, and for yet another person, love may mean hearing the right words in the right way, or getting presents, or getting married.

Don't make the mistake of assuming you know what the other person's definition of love is. Ask. And keep asking. You'll get more than one answer. To get to the best answer, use a line of questioning like this:

Q: How do you know you're loved?
A: When I feel in partnership.
Q: How do you know when you are in partnership?
A: When I'm sharing something with another person.

This way, you may elicit four or five values connected with love alone, and you can use the technique you learned a few pages ago to encourage others to put their values in order of importance.

Q LT *THEOREM*

DISCOVERING THE HIERARCHY OF VALUES IS THE FIRST STEP. CLARIFYING THE MEANING IS THE SECOND STEP.

Understanding your values and creating a personal vision statement is not enough to make that quantum leap. You have to act.

If your highest value is relationships and you have a fear of rejection, you will probably move away from what you need most. If your number-one value is achievement, and you have a terrible fear of failure, you will undoubtedly avoid the very thing that can make you feel complete.

Your brain is constantly evaluating, judging, weighing, and juggling alternatives. During this process, the pain you associate with certain emotions will influence your decision making. You will move away from choices that may cause you humiliation, guilt, anger, rejection, failure, frustration, or loneliness.

> You cannot run away from a weakness; you must sometimes fight it out or perish. And if that is so, why not now, and where you stand?
>
> —ROBERT LOUIS STEVENSON,
> Scottish author

It's vitally important to become conscious of your personal demons. They create powerlessness and purposelessness. If there is a fear directly connected to your top core value, you have a real conflict. Which is stronger? Push or pull? Move away or toward? You sabotage yourself when you don't know why you do what you do.

Curiously, most of us put more energy into avoiding pain than into pursuing pleasure. To avoid a values conflict, we must clearly see what causes us the greatest amount of pain.

Think about powerful negative emotions, those you passionately wish to avoid, like jealousy, loneliness, lack of self-esteem, failure, rejection, powerlessness, or boredom. You should be able to come up with three that make your own brand of unhappiness.

Now, remember how your values were created. Family, society, peers, teachers, and environment helped mold and shape who you are and what your values are. No one sat you down with a checklist of values and asked you to choose the ones you wanted.

Think about your list of painful emotions together with your list of values and see if there is any conflict. If so, you need to replace the marble in your value kaleidoscope.

Take some quiet time and brainstorm with yourself. Are your values out of date? Are there new values that are more appropriate to your current experience and knowledge? Is there a value that would put your life more in balance? Do you need to reframe how you view your fears?

If you change your choice or order of values, give yourself a day or two and do a reality check. If you're comfortable with your decision, commit to it. View your life through the lens of your new value structure and act accordingly.

> We are what we repeatedly do.
> —ARISTOTLE,
> Greek philosopher

Now for the most difficult challenge: *consciously living your values.* Most of us are blind to it. We may say our family, friends, or relationships come first, but then commit our time and energy to work, hobbies, sports, or social functions. Then we are dismayed to find our lives are out of balance.

Do you commit your resources of time and money to those things you say are your highest values? Talk is cheap; actions are everything.

Your core values give you a personal compass to guide you in your daily decision-making process. When your decisions come from the very structure of what you value, you not only live with integrity, but you also live with commitment and passion.

QUANTUM LEAP VALUES

Part of my chosen life's work is to help people become aware of their values and provide strategies so they can form their personal and organizational visions. But what if they lack personal integrity? What if they have no sense of fair play? What if they are greedy and self-serving, and don't care how their actions impact others? What if they use the tools I teach them to manipulate others, to achieve an end where the greatest number of people lose?

Much of the world's history was created by effective motivation. Hundreds of dictators and tyrants are proof of that. Didn't a sense of dedication, commitment, and loyalty play a role in the power of their visions? What about street gangs, motorcycle gangs, and skinheads? They have a value structure.

But this book is about improving quality of life, and if you are committed to making quantum leaps in your personal growth, it is not enough to simply have values, know what they are, and live by them. If you want to create a fulfilling and motivated life for yourself and for others, if you want to play the biggest game of

> In order to reach the highest level possible in your personal or organizational life, there are specific global principles, or core values, that must become part of your Grand Vision.

all, the game of possibility, you must have—and act from—the five core values of a Quantum Leap Thinker.

■ THE FIVE QUANTUM LEAP VALUES

QLT Value #1: Respect.

Having respect for the dignity of the individual is the single most important QLT Value. This governs the way you communicate with and the way you see and experience people. This essential value acts as a springboard to charity, compassion, fairness, and service.

As you challenge your traditional ways of thinking, you will discover, exponentially, your connection to the world around you and your need for interdependence. As you break out of your self-created illusion of separateness, you will, as Einstein said, "widen your circle of compassion to embrace all living creatures and the whole of nature in its beauty."

From the awareness of our interconnectedness flows compassion and empathy. Respect for the dignity of the individual is the antidote to prejudice, jealousy, envy, manipulation, and deceit.

QLT Value #2: Accountability.

> Do what you feel in your heart to be right—for you'll be criticized anyway. You'll be damned if you do, and damned if you don't.
>
> —ELEANOR ROOSEVELT

My brother, Dave, is a junior high school teacher. With his own children and with his students, he teaches a very simple principle: You have unlimited choices and you may choose to do whatever you like to do, as long as you are willing to pay the price.

I like that.

Accountability opens up your personal freedom, but at the same time drives home cause and effect. Being accountable defuses the mythical "they did it" excuse. "They forgot to tell me." "They messed up the works." "They have all the good jobs."

Freedom must be accompanied by accountability. By making accountability a major value in your Grand Vision, you take the leap from being a victim to being a player. In the final analysis, accountability places your destiny in your hands.

QLT Value #3: Integrity.

One of the definitions of integrity in *Webster's New World Dictionary* goes beyond the obvious meanings of honesty and sincerity. Integrity is defined as "completeness, wholeness or an unimpaired condition."

Architects and builders use the phrase "structural integrity" when referring to the solidity of a building. I feel the same concept can be applied to the solidity of a human being. The greater our personal integrity, the greater our completeness and wholeness.

Integrity means being congruent with what you say and what you do. My father used to say, "Don't do as I do; do as I say." He was kidding, but that is exactly how many people operate.

Do your actions match your words? This is the first element of integrity. Do your actions match your values? This is the second element of integrity.

It is deceptively easy to lie. We may lie to protect someone, or so we don't hurt people's feelings, or because we think it is for their own good. Lies are told out of fear; lies are told to manipulate; lies are told when we bargain. The reasons we invent for lying are endless.

You may, at this very moment, be thinking that there are in fact necessary lies, little white lies. I've certainly told my share. But regardless of how compelling the reasons, a lie is never justified.

Choosing to live with integrity is a private, personal, and powerful choice. Truth is your weapon against Fear, the Great Trickster.

QLT Value #4: Perseverance.

> Press on. Nothing in the world can take the place of perseverance. Talent will not; nothing is more common than unsuccessful men with talent. Genius will not; unrewarded genius is almost a proverb. Education will not; the world is full of educated derelicts. Persistence and determination alone are omnipotent.
>
> —CALVIN COOLIDGE,
> thirtieth president of the United States

Perseverance must be instilled in childhood, or else the retraining process will consume valuable time. Susan Granger, my other half and my greatest support, told me a story. When she was a little girl, her father would ask her, "What did you accomplish today?"

If she had abandoned something because she was discouraged or distracted, she was reminded each night at dinner of her mission: to accomplish something each day. Her father's daily interest in her progress embedded deep within her the value of accomplishment, of perseverance, a characteristic she exhibits today. To please her father, and ultimately to please herself, she persevered.

QLT Value #5: Discipline.

> No pain, no palm; no thorns, no throne; no gall, no glory; no cross, no crown.
>
> —WILLIAM PENN,
> English Quaker and founder of Pennsylvania

People want the simple and easy way, but as the great Prussian military strategist Carl von Clausewitz said, "Simple and easy are not synonymous." The irony is that there is often a greater expenditure of energy in the attempt to make things easy than to just do the job in the first place.

In 1972, for example, I began to work out with weights. Quite frankly, it's not a lot of fun, but I had a vision of what I could look like, and there wasn't any shortcut to look like that. Over the years I completely transformed myself from an overweight, soft, self-conscious person to somebody rather fit and strong. There still lingers the shadow of my former self, that chubby kid, but that negative memory just strengthens my commitment to exercise. I want to feel good. I want to look good. I am committed to it. So I go to the gym. I don't even think about it; I just go. In short, I have developed the discipline to work out.

Discipline is more than following procedures. Procedures imply following orders; discipline is a personal choice. Discipline and commitment go hand-in-hand. The difference is the difference between compliance or commitment; stopping when the going gets rough or plowing through with energy; settling for mediocrity or striving for excellence. Just because you do your job doesn't mean you're committed to the job you're doing.

The five Quantum Leap Thinking Values come into play only after you have taken the time to create your own hierarchy of values. Review your original value hierarchy: Do you wish to replace any of your six values with any of the Quantum Leap Values?

▓ STAYING ON THE RIGHT TRACK

My grandfather drove a steam engine, and as a young boy all I ever dreamed about was to be like him, controlling the Iron Horse. I remember the blast of heat from the furnace against my face as I watched two muscular, sweating men shovel coal into the fiery hole. Most of the time I rode in the engineer's cabin, watching Grandpa work the levers that controlled the steam pressure with the deft skill of a musician. With my fingers tightly plugged in my ears, I imagined myself in his place, manipulating the long, shiny brass handles, periodically releasing loud blasts of steam.

He controlled our speed with total concentration and sensitivity as we coupled up with or released cars at various locations. Sometimes I felt we were moving at the pace of a snail. At other times, free of the burden of dragging the massive weight of many cars behind the engine, we flew along the tracks. Grandpa let me blast the horn. I loved the immense power of that machine and eagerly awaited the surprise of our destinations.

One night Grandpa sat me on his lap and, placing his large

hands over my small ones, taught me to play the tune of those brass handles. Together, we rerouted the Iron Horse from one track to another, gently guided it into the roundhouse, and put that big beast to bed for the night.

Creating a vision is like operating that train. It often requires rerouting to a different track, and we must be flexible enough to adjust the pressure to increase or decrease our speed and to know how to throw the proper switches to change direction at a moment's notice. We may need to make unexpected stops and detours along the way. Those stops and detours are a necessary part of the journey. We may need them to refocus, examine our values, and balance our lives.

THE MIND BY MAPES

You may derive thoughts from others; your way of thinking, the
mould in which your thoughts are cast must be your own.
—CHARLES LAMB,
English essayist

According to Freudian theory, the mind is composed of the
id, ego, and superego. The psychologist Abraham Maslow
looked at the mind as integrated, rather than separate, parts.
Many people acknowledge a conscious and a subconscious, and
others believe there is no division in the mind whatsoever.

I choose to divide the mind into three parts: the Conscious
Mind, the Creative Mind, and the Subconscious Mind.

THE CONSCIOUS MIND

Only crazy people hear voices.
—Anonymous

The Conscious Mind is that little voice in your head that talks to
you. If you don't know what little voice I'm referring to, it's the

one that is asking right now, "What little voice is he talking about?" It's your "self-talk" or what I refer to as "mind-chatter." This voice is constantly judging, analyzing, rationalizing, and commenting. This voice reflects your values and belief system. It is the montage of your conditioning and learning, both negative and positive. The majority of your mind-chatter replays the outdated voices of parents, friends, and teachers.

You have the capability to direct your conscious mind. You can create positive, healthy, empowering self-talk that reinforces and builds your self-esteem. Using the conscious mind, you can write and speak affirmations to support your goals. You can summon the power of your imagination to create and direct pictures of an ideal future.

The challenge is to discern the difference between positive and negative self-talk. Once you become aware of the difference, you can choose to let go of the negative and focus on the most nurturing and empowering.

> One of the ways that creative people in business exemplify the "don't-think-about-it" credo is by refusing to dwell on past mistakes or future worries.
> —MICHAEL RAY AND ROCHELLE MYERS,
> *Creativity in Business*

Are you aware of the "worry wars" that go on in your conscious mind? You take one point of view in a self-conversation, only to switch to another point of view with its own set of rationalizations and justifications, and then you might even switch to a third. Each time you switch, of course, you are right. These are the worry wars.

Worry is a self-perpetuating cycle that creates enormous stress. When you are caught up in a worry war, creative, proactive choice ceases to exist, and it's a difficult habit to break.

How do you stop? Once you're aware of it, blast yourself with a thought or voice louder than the voice of worry. Just yell, "Stop!" Sounds silly, but it works.

> Drag your thoughts away from your troubles by the ear, by the heels, or any other way, so you manage it; it's the healthiest thing a body can do.
> —MARK TWAIN,
> American novelist

When you are aware of self-talk and worry wars, you will begin to notice specific, self-limiting language, words like *can't, impossible, try, should, could,* and *would,* words that must be eliminated from your thinking. Create positive self-talk, or affirmations, that support your goals.

> Judge thyself with the judgment of sincerity, and thou will judge others with the judgment of charity.
> —JOHN MITCHELL MASON,
> nineteenth-century clergyman and
> president of Dickinson College

Make developing awareness a project for yourself. Pay attention to your thinking. Become aware of your "voice of judgment," because judgment is a creativity killer. Notice when you judge something or somebody as wrong or stupid, or an idea as silly or impossible. A major step to Quantum Leap Thinking is understanding that you are *at choice* in your thinking process. You can choose to quiet the destructive voices in your mind.

QLT *THEOREM*

YOU CHOOSE YOUR THOUGHTS MOMENT TO MOMENT. AWARENESS OF YOUR POWER TO CHOOSE GIVES YOU THE FREEDOM TO CHOOSE ANEW.

THE CREATIVE MIND

> The majority of business people are incapable of original thought because they are unable to escape the tyranny of reason.
> —DAVID OGILVY,
> CEO, Ogilvy & Mather

Like most students, I waited until the night before an exam to do the major portion of my studying. I joined other students to cram until the wee hours of the morning. By the time I fell asleep, my mind was a confusing jumble of facts. I worried about my ability to remember the time and place of the exam, let alone the information I needed to pass.

The next day I would sit down at my desk filled with a sense of dread. Yet when the exam was passed out, the answers flowed forth like magic. The information had somehow organized itself in spite of my confusion.

I learned to trust this mysterious process, sure that I had discovered a secret that was unique to me. I used this skill whenever I felt confused about something. I would write the problem on paper before I went to sleep. When I woke up, usually a solution had taken shape.

Now I know this process is not unique to me. We all have the capability to use that part of our mind that seeks out solutions. The key is being able to state the problem, allow time to pass, and trust there will be an answer forthcoming. This is the three-part idea-generation process mentioned in practically every book on creative thinking:

1. Information gathering.
2. Incubation.
3. Outcome.

Learning to use the creative mind is like baking bread. To make bread, my mother would combine the ingredients, knead the dough, place it in a pan, set it aside, and trust the yeast to do its job. The bread would then rise and be ready for baking. She knew the outcome she wanted, and the formula for getting it done, and she had the patience to see the process to completion. She knew she couldn't hurry the process.

Similarly, if you know what you want to achieve, do your research, let the information sit a while (like bread rising), trust, and are patient, the answer will usually, miraculously, appear.

Q L T *THEOREM*

PUTTING PRESSURE ON THE CREATIVE MIND TO PRODUCE WILL ALWAYS CUT OFF THE CREATIVE PROCESS. TRUST ALLOWS THE RESULT TO OCCUR NATURALLY.

The conscious mind gives you specific control by the use of affirmations and positive self-talk. You can learn to reframe your thinking. You can substitute a positive thought for the negative.

The creative mind provides you with a resource for problem solving and idea generation.

But it is the subconscious mind that holds the magic to shift your reality and take the quantum leap.

■ THE SUBCONSCIOUS MIND

> It is quite possible to overcome infantile suggestions of the unconscious, and even to change the contents of the unconscious, by employing the right kind of technique. . . . Let your conscious beliefs be so vivid and emphatic that they make an impression upon your unconscious.
> —BERTRAND RUSSELL,
> English philosopher

A computer that could match the power of the human mind is highly unlikely, but the metaphor of the subconscious mind as a computer is used by many psychologists, and after working more than twenty years in the field of hypnosis and visualization, I can't think of a better one.

Recall for a moment the two hypnosis demonstrations I described in Chapter 7. The first created a belief that paper money was too heavy to pick up. The second eliminated a given number in the subject's mind. If you program the subconscious, the result will always be a direct reflection of the quality of the programming.

There are even more incredible hypnosis demonstrations of altered reality and new behavior. Clinically hypnosis can help eliminate or reduce pain. Athletes can improve their strength, dexterity, concentration, coordination, and speed. A clinical hypnotist can teach a subject to tap into the power of his or her subconscious mind to stop smoking or lose weight.

My specialty in the field of clinical hypnosis was age regression. For some years I worked with police departments to help victims of or witnesses to crimes retrieve forgotten or suppressed information. I worked with victims of child abuse to help them understand and forgive what had happened to them. I saw challenge in being a detective of the mind.

The subconscious mind has meticulously recorded all experiences. Given the appropriate conditions and willingness of the subject, any experience can be retrieved in its entirety. If the experience is negative, it can be transformed by reprogramming to be positive. The subject then shifts his or her paradigm. The result can be magical. As strange as hypnosis may seem, it is nothing more than creating a shift in the subconscious mind.

There are four aspects of the subconscious mind to remember:

1. The subconscious mind does not think. It is only a storehouse of our experiences.
2. There is no sense of time in the subconscious mind.
3. The subconscious mind cannot differentiate between positive or negative input.
4. The subconscious mind cannot tell the difference between a real or an imagined experience.

It is the fourth attribute of the subconscious that gives us the power to control our thinking and create our destiny.

QLT *THEOREM*

THE SUBCONSCIOUS MIND CANNOT TELL THE DIFFERENCE BETWEEN A REAL OR AN IMAGINED EXPERIENCE.

Think of a lemon. Recall its shape, its texture, its pungent smell. Now imagine slicing the lemon in half. In your mind, pick up one of the halves and look at it, squeeze it, and watch the juice spurt out. Imagine bringing the lemon slowly toward your mouth. Now imagine taking a big, juicy bite. Did you have a reaction?

Now take half of a real lemon and ask a few family members or friends to imagine biting it while you actually bite into the lemon. Their reaction will be as strong and immediate as yours.

Ninety percent of us experience a biochemical response in our mouths by simply imagining the act of biting a lemon. Consider what this means: A biochemical response is created out of pure illusion—something from nothing.

If you had a response to the thought of biting a lemon, you did it with the power of your imagination. If you ask others to imagine taking a bite from a lemon and they have a reaction, you guided their imagination, but they created their own reaction.

The subconscious reads the imagined experience as real. If you can create that kind of response by conjuring up a lemon in your imagination, consider that you may have an effect on your immune system by how you think. Consider how you might affect the immune system of others through your communication. In medical terms, the phenomenon is called psychoneuroimmunology. Clinical studies of the mind have shown that our thoughts have a direct impact on our health. The mind and the body are inseparable. It's truly all in the mind.

Think about something negative—being rejected, failing at a task, losing money, getting fired, having an accident. If you created a vivid picture in your mind, you will feel it in your body.

Now imagine yourself being welcomed with open arms, succeeding at work, winning a lottery ticket. Can you physically feel the difference between negative and positive thought?

If you created an emotionally charged image of yourself in a negative situation and then changed that image to a positive one, you noticed a distinct change in the way you felt.

Q LT *THEOREM*

IMAGERY IS THE LANGUAGE OF THE SUBCONSCIOUS.

> Mental imagery is remarkably able to substitute for actual perception. Subjects make the same judgments about objects in their absence as in their presence.
> —DR. ROGER N. SHEPARD,
> *American psychologist*

I'm often on the road for weeks at a time, and one of the great joys of my life is to come home and walk in the woods with my dogs. Even as I write this, I feel good. But if I imagine one of my dogs hit by a car and killed, I can feel my body spiral downward into a deep state of sadness.

I imagined a negative future; my physical self did the rest. Like the lemon, a mental image will cause the mind to react as if faced by the real thing. The power of visualization, of mental imaging, is one of the most effective tools you have.

> However mean your life is, meet it and live it; do not shun and call it hard names. It is not so bad as you are. It looks poorest when you are richest. The fault-finder will find faults even in Paradise. Love your life.
>
> —HENRY DAVID THOREAU

Consider the following: Outside of physical violence, no one does anything to you. No one makes you feel angry, depressed, jealous, or defensive. Those feelings are responses to situations you feel you can't control. They stem from the primitive "fight or flight" mechanism.

People, situations, and things don't make us angry; we get angry. People, situations, and things don't make us depressed; we get depressed. We generate our emotional reactions.

I am not suggesting that fear-based emotions are wrong. They come from a childlike place within us that wants things to be the way we want them to be. We often feel out of control when our expectations are not met. This is a natural reaction. But being accountable to and responsible for our emotions can make a great difference to our mental and physical health. When we own our emotions, we become proactive. We cease to blame or play the victim.

REACTIVE

NO OWNERSHIP
(victim, blame,
resistance, guilt)

PROACTIVE

OWNERSHIP
(I'm part of the problem and
part of the solution.)

THE QUANTUM LEAP

The first of our senses which we should take care never to let rust through disuse is that sixth sense, the imagination. I mean the wide-open eye which leads us always to see truth more vividly, to comprehend more broadly, to concern ourselves more deeply, to be, all our life long, sensitive and awake to the powers and responsibilities given to us as human beings.

—CHRISTOPHER FRY,
English playwright

■ THE QUANTUM LEAP THINKING PENDULUM

Find a length of string (kite twine or thread will do) and cut it to approximately ten inches in length. Attach some kind of weight to one end: a ring, a key, or a small metal washer.

Hold the end of the string, allowing the weight to hang down about four inches above the center of the circle below. Don't let your elbow rest on a surface while you hold the string.

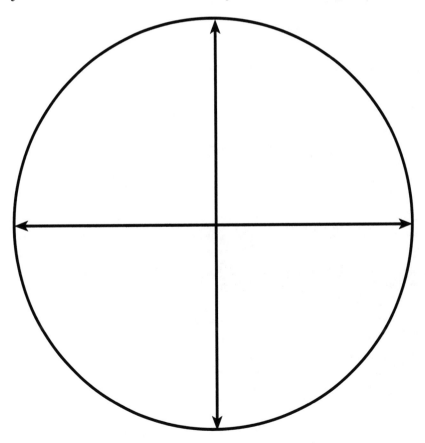

Now momentarily focus your attention on the horizontal line. *Imagine* the weight moving back and forth, left to right. Think left . . . right . . . left . . . right. Feel the pendulum swinging back and forth . . . left and right. See it in your mind's eye, moving left and right as if it were already happening. The pendulum will begin to move exactly as you imagine it moving.

Change your thought. Now imagine the pendulum moving in a circle. Imagine the circle becoming larger, and the movement will follow your thought.

Now take your other hand and hold the wrist of the hand holding the string. Continue imagining the pendulum moving in a circle. Even though you are holding your wrist, the movement doesn't stop, because your entire body is in motion. The proof of that statement is in the movement of the string.

Q LT *THEOREM*

YOU WILL ALWAYS MOVE IN THE DIRECTION OF YOUR THOUGHTS.

Why does the pendulum move? When you have a thought, neurons fire in the brain, creating small electrical charges. When the charges hit the central nervous system, a corresponding internal and external reaction takes place, creating movement.

This is an oversimplification of a very complex physiological process, but essentially that is what happens: A thought within the brain triggers a physical reaction in the body.

Now you understand how your thoughts affect your entire physiology—your blood pressure, stress level, heart rate, and even your golf swing. The way you choose to think affects every aspect of your life. The way you think literally guides your body in the direction of the thought.

For years the belief that the mind affects the body was viewed as eccentric, but hard evidence compiled from years of careful research is so overwhelming that it can no longer be denied. How we think, the belief systems we hold, and how we use our imagination vitally impact our lives at every given moment, on every level, waking or sleeping.

I really enjoy watching a group of corporate executives do the pendulum exercise. It provides the platform for the most stubborn group to discover, as a unit, the power of the imagination. The power of this collective discovery immediately energizes everyone with curiosity. With a piece of string and a weight, anyone can experience the incredible power of the imagination.

> The world of reality has its limits; the world of imagination is boundless. Not being able to enlarge the one, let us contract the other; for it is from their difference that all the evils arise which render us unhappy.
>
> —JEAN-JACQUES ROUSSEAU,
> French philosopher and writer

I used to love reading comic books. On the back page of one of my favorites I discovered an advertisement for the most amazing electronic set I had ever seen. With it I could make all kinds of things, even a radio! I was so excited I could hardly wait to show my parents.

My enthusiasm convinced my mother and father, and together we planned how I could pay for it out of my allowance. I filled out the order form, enclosed the payment, and carried it to the post office myself.

When the coveted package finally arrived, I brought it up to my room, opened the box, and unwrapped hundreds of pieces of electronic paraphernalia sealed in plastic bags, a coiled roll of solder, and a soldering iron.

I was dumbfounded. I stared at the array of equipment, deeply discouraged and bitterly disappointed. To this day I'm not exactly sure what I had expected. Somehow the advertisement led me to believe that I could have all those magical items presented as complete in the ad, without investing a lot of work.

I suspect the expectations of people searching for life's answers fall into a similar trap. Buy a book, attend a lecture, or listen to a tape and *poof*! Everything will fall into place instantly, without strategy, commitment, patience, or action. Somehow we all get deluded into believing there is a shortcut to mastery.

Fortunately it is not that easy. I say "fortunately" because it is the *process* that is exciting. I didn't realize that when I unwrapped my electronics kit, but when my dad and I worked together and built magical things, I realized it then.

Becoming a Quantum Leap Thinker involves a whole lot of work, but I am confident that you will discover that putting together the pieces of the "kit" is the best part of the game. The fun begins with an understanding of how we create the images that govern our reality. The greatest gift we possess is the power of our imagination.

> Imagination is more important than knowledge.
>
> —ALBERT EINSTEIN

TAKING THE LEAP

POSITIVE VISUALIZATION: THE POWER WITHIN

Take charge of your thoughts. You can do what you
want with them.

—PLATO,
Greek philosopher

Visualization is the process of creating a clear, sharp, emotionally charged mental movie of what you want to happen, imagining events as if they have already happened. Visualization is a mental rehearsal of things to come, so you can better handle them when they do. Visualization has become a trendy concept for an old practice.

More than two thousand years ago the poet Virgil wrote, "Mind moves matter." Harnessing the power of the mind has long been a part of folk wisdom, from the teachings of Zen masters to playing the inner game of tennis or golf.

Nearly sixty years ago British psychologist Edmund Jacobson demonstrated that thought actually has a direct physiological effect on the body. He connected a complicated measuring device to various muscles in a man's body, and then asked the man to think about running. Although the man was at rest, every muscle connected with running moved.

Stanford University neurophysiologist Karl Pribram's revealing research on what he refers to as the "Holographic Brain" confirmed that an image created in the mind fires the same neural connections in the autonomic nervous system as does the act. Thinking and doing, insofar as the autonomic nervous system is concerned, are the same. Remember, the subconscious mind cannot tell the difference between a real and an imagined experience.

Several case studies have confirmed how visualization has provided remarkable results. A concert pianist and former prisoner of war reported practicing on an imaginary keyboard every day he was in prison. Upon his release he was able to play the piano as if he had actually practiced. Another POW visualized himself playing a round of golf every day on one of his favorite courses. Shortly after his release he scored one of the best rounds of golf he has ever played.

Dr. Charles Garfield, psychology professor at the University of California at San Francisco Medical School, president of the Peak Performance Center near Berkeley, former NASA scientist and power-lifter, wrote in his book *Peak Performers,* "The key to success in all walks of life is picturing or visualizing the exact, precise way you want an event to go."

FORTIS IMAGINATIO GENERAT CAUSUM
(A strong imagination begets the event itself)

A classic experiment proving the power of visualization took place in a Chicago physical education class. Three groups of basketball players were told that they had a month to prepare for a contest consisting of twenty free-throws. Group A was told to practice shooting one hundred free-throws a day for thirty days, Group B was told to practice as they would normally, and Group C was told not to practice at all. However, Group C was instructed to spend fifteen minutes every day visualizing shooting perfect free-throws.

At the end of the month Group A, the group that had actually practiced, and Group C, the group that had only visualized their success, had essentially the same scores. Group B lost dramatically. Imagine the results if you combine actual practice with visualization. The power of performance is ignited with the fuel of visualization.

In *Golf My Way,* Jack Nicklaus writes,

> I never hit a shot, even in practice, without having a very sharp, in-focus picture of it in my head. It's like a color movie. First I see the ball where I want it to finish, nice and white and sitting up high on the bright green grass. Then the scene quickly changes and I see the ball going there: its path, trajectory, and shape, even its behavior on landing. Then there's a sort of fade-out, and the next scene shows me making the kind of swing that will turn the previous images into reality. Only at the end of this short, private Hollywood spectacular do I select a club and step up to the ball.

If you're like most golfers, you probably plant your feet and set the club behind the ball before giving a thought to what you are going to do. If you want to see your score improve, do what Nicklaus does.

Shamans and folk healers around the world consider the imagination as the key to unlocking self-healing powers. Yet the majority of the Western world's medical professions have not yet accepted the mind as a scientific tool.

Dr. O. Carl Simonton, a radiation oncologist, and his wife, psychologist Stephanie Matthews-Simonton, were visionaries. Their work using visualization with cancer patients stirred great debate in the 1970s. In their book *Getting Well Again,* the Simontons claimed that the immune function could be boosted by visualizing strong white blood cells attacking weak cancer cells.

Dr. Simonton learned about the power of imagery while he was serving as a doctor in the Air Force. He noticed that a number of cancer patients who were considered medically hopeless not only survived but seemed to reverse the course of their disease. He noticed a marked difference in attitude between those whose health improved and those whose health did not. The patients who saw themselves as fighters survived longer than did those who viewed themselves as victims.

Dr. Simonton's curiosity led him to consider the possibility that changing a patient's negative self-image and attitude would affect the progression of the cancer.

The first stage of the Simontons' treatment involved educating patients about their disease. The second stage taught relaxation and visualization techniques. He asked patients to visualize good, cancer-fighting cells with strong, tough, aggressive, disease-killing imagery, such as sharks, knights in shining armor, or jet fighter pilots. Then he told them to visualize the cancer cells as puny, weak, and vulnerable, being attacked and devoured by the healthy cells.

The Simontons' initial research involved 159 patients, each with a prognosis of a year or less. Of those patients who incorporated visualization with more traditional forms of cancer therapy, 19 percent eliminated their cancer completely, 22 percent went into remission, and those who finally succumbed to the disease on average doubled their predicted survival time. While visualization alone may not conquer cancer, imagining killer cells does help kick in a whole host of biological processes that lead to healing. As respected physicians, the Simontons opened the door to further scientific exploration as to how visualization can directly impact the immune system.

In a 1983 experiment at Michigan State University, students were taught to control specific functions of certain white blood cells. Students in the experiment caused an average of 60 percent of their neutrophils (white blood cells that engulf foreign particles) to exit the bloodstream and enter the surrounding tissue.

These experiments and even more recent work in the field of the mind/body relationship have given birth to the relatively new field of psychoneuroimmunology. Even the most basic research has generated a significant body of evidence that the way we think does make a difference on the body.

While many doctors stubbornly cling to traditional methods, it seems foolhardy to ignore the simple, proven fact that what goes on in our minds has a dramatic impact on our bodies.

Q LT *THEOREM*

NO THOUGHT, NO EMOTION IS WITHOUT BIOCHEMICAL AND ELECTROCHEMICAL ACTIVITY, AND THIS ACTIVITY LEAVES NO CELL UNTOUCHED.

Pretend, for the moment, that you want to go on a Colorado skiing trip. Make a clear mental picture of that goal. Visualize the snow-capped mountains and the picturesque chalet where you will stay. See yourself in the chalet, looking out over the crisp, white snow. Feel yourself skiing down the slope, exhilarated.

How well you visualize depends a great deal on how well your mind has been trained. Some of us can create pictures as complete as a feature film, in living color, full of sound and detail and in 3-D. If at first your movie is vague, don't despair. Visualization takes practice.

Think about the lemon again. Just a second or two of visualizing the act of biting into it created a physiological reaction in your mouth. You may have even shuddered.

Now imagine yourself on vacation, sitting under a palm tree on a sandy beach, watching a plane take off. Or imagine yourself in a drenching rainstorm or watching a fire engine race down a street. You are able to create realities in your mind without moving from where you are. You have the power to do that. You can control your thoughts.

> This is not so mystical as it may first appear. You and I do it every day of our lives. What, for example, is worry about possible unfavorable results, accompanied by feelings of anxiety, inadequacy, or perhaps humiliation? For all practical purposes, we experience the very same emotions in advance that would be appropriate if we had already failed. We picture failure to ourselves, not vaguely, or in personal terms, but vividly and in great detail. We repeat the failure images over and over again to ourselves.
>
> —DR. MAXWELL MALTZ,
> author, *PsychoCybernetics*

Consciously using the visualization process is like using electricity; you don't have to know how it works to get a result. Your power is already there. You don't even have to turn it on; you only have to direct it.

> Imagination rules the world.
>
> —NAPOLÉON BONAPARTE,
> French emperor

Q LT *THEOREM*

THE SPEED WITH WHICH YOU ACHIEVE YOUR GOALS DIRECTLY RE-LATES TO HOW CLEARLY AND HOW OFTEN YOU VISUALIZE THEM.

Did you ever play with magnets when you were a child? I remember my delight when I could push one magnet around the tabletop with the force of another. With a mere twist of the wrist, I could pull the magnet back.

The mental pictures you create work in much the same way. When I create a mental movie of what an overwhelming job it will be to write a book, I do everything I can to avoid writing. If I visualize the work in small, manageable sections and see each one complete, I look forward to writing. If I add joy and satisfaction to the picture, I add real power to the process. When I see the book as bound, published, and on the shelves of bookstores, I get a real burst of energy.

> Unless there be correct thought, there cannot be any action; and when there is correct thought, the right action follows.
>
> —HENRY GEORGE,
> American economist

Suppose you are postponing doing a report or preparing a speech. The reason for your procrastination may be the way you see your future. Pictures of failure, disaster, or insurmountable obstacles probably whirl around in your mental movie of the future. You might justify putting it off by reasoning that you work better under pressure or that the task will be easier at a later date. The pictures create movement away from your goal. One magnet is repelling the other. Simply turn the magnet around.

> There is a law in psychology that if you form a picture in your mind of what you would like to be, and you keep and hold that picture there long enough, you will soon become exactly as you have been thinking.
>
> —WILLIAM JAMES,
> American philosopher

Define for yourself the feelings and emotions connected with an ideal future. Elation? Satisfaction? Relief? The more your future picture is filled with enticing, attractive possibilities, the more power and energy you have to move toward a positive outcome. The magnet reverses. When the dream is grand enough, incredible amounts of energy surface. Whether it's selling a new product, starting a new business, or writing a report, the way you visualize the outcome determines the direction, ease, and speed with which you move.

Q L T *THEOREM*

YOU CREATE YOUR REALITY TWICE: FIRST IN YOUR IMAGINATION AND THEN IN THE WORLD.

Whether you believe in the power of visualization or choose to use it won't affect the fact that you already visualize constantly. Your life is the result of how you think. Just like your body and the pendulum, a mental picture creates a corresponding response. Empowering thoughts create empowering behavior. Negative thoughts create negative behavior.

BENCH RACING: VISUALIZATION IN ACTION

Some friends and I decided that it would be a great adventure to go to the Grand Prix race car driving school. We compared calendars and schedules and sent in our applications for a three-day training session.

The night before our first class, we met for dinner, imagined ourselves driving at breakneck speeds, and went to bed excited. The next morning we were given sleek blue racing suits and colorful helmets. We were fired up and ready to get in our cars.

But it wasn't quite that simple. Our instructor told us we would be doing a lot of bench racing.

"What's bench racing?" I asked him.

"Sitting on the bench and imagining driving your car around the track."

A disappointed hush fell over the room. All we wanted to do was get out on the track and drive fast.

"The key to being a successful race car driver," the instructor continued, "is directly related to your ability to bench race. You will mentally rehearse braking, downshifting, and steering long before you run the course and immediately thereafter. Correct your mistakes when you are off the track, because there is no time to do it when you're flying around curves. If you don't take the time to bench race, you will repeat the same mistakes over and over again. And believe me, at the speed you'll be driving, you won't have the time to think. Take advantage of your time off the track."

I can't tell you how right he was. On the second day I barely avoided smashing headlong into a brick wall. I lost control and, mesmerized by the wall in front of me, went into a skid. While whirling around in a spin, I sheared both the front and back ends of the car off. I climbed out, shaking in terror.

I was immediately assigned another car and sent out on the same track. I was truly terrified. The mental picture of hitting the wall kept playing over and over in my mind. I drove with the speed of a snail.

My instructor told me to take some time out and bench race. I found an empty seat on the sidelines, closed my eyes, and deliberately ran a new script in my mind. I saw myself executing the necessary moves to make the turn. I went back out on the track with my heart pounding and my instructor's voice ringing in my ears: "Don't look where you don't want to go."

The wind whipped so hard against the face mask of my helmet that my neck muscles were strained. I was rapidly approaching my nemesis. This time, however, just like I had rehearsed on the bench, I gently hit the brakes, downshifted, and fought the steering wheel. I went into the turn, double-clutched, shifted, and flew into the straightaway perfectly. My speed climbed. Rounding the next corner, I got the flag. I came in second out of six.

The old reflexes are still pretty good, I thought to myself, but I knew it was bench racing that had saved me.

▌QLT▐ *THEOREM*

EVENTS MOVE TOO FAST FOR YOU TO MAKE YOUR COURSE CORRECTION WHILE YOU ARE IN MOTION. VISUALIZE THE EVENTS EXACTLY AS YOU DESIRE THEM TO BE BEFORE THE ACTION.

Images and mental pictures . . . tend to produce the physical conditions and external acts that correspond to them.
—ROBERTO ASSAGIOLI,
The Act of Will

One of the most positive learning experiences I have had using the power of visualization took place on an Outward Bound adventure. Eleven of us were invited to go on a seven-day rafting trip down the Green River in Utah. The people in charge had scheduled a slew of challenging activities, one of which was a rock climb. And I don't like heights.

Our instructor gave us a little education about climbing techniques and a long list of safety tips. He kept reminding us to see ourselves at the top. He said the subconscious has the amazing ability to guide us in finding the way up as long as we could envision ourselves already there. He had us stand at the bottom, studying the rock face for about ten minutes, before the first of our group began the climb. I watched.

It didn't look easy. The thought of searching out minuscule toe- and fingerholds in the sheer face of a rock cliff did not make my heart soar with confidence.

Suddenly it was my turn. The instructor strapped me in a harness, and I began to climb. It wasn't nearly as difficult as I thought it would be until I got about three-quarters up the face. I couldn't find a fingerhold. I was bearing the entire weight of my body on the toes of my left foot. I continued to poke around in the rocks with mounting desperation. I begin to feel dizzy. People were yelling instructions to me, but I couldn't focus on what they were saying. All I could think was, *I'm going to fall. I'm going to fall.*

One leg was shaking so hard I thought I had developed palsy. *It would be so easy to just let go.*

The instructor's voice blasted in my mind. "See yourself at the top!"

At that moment I was able to form a clear, vivid picture of myself standing at the top of the cliff. Then the magic happened. I felt as though I was in an altered state; I discovered the fingerhold I needed. One movement after another—toe, hand, toe, hand—and I felt myself being pulled by helping hands. It was an extraordinary experience.

"Don't fall. Don't drop that. Don't get hit by a car when you're crossing the street. Don't hit the ball into the sand trap. Don't feel rejected."

All these statements have one thing in common: They are powerful suggestions to the subconscious to do exactly what they warn against. Your behavior is controlled by the part of the mind that works in pictures, and that part of the mind hears, "Fall down. Be rejected. Get hit by a car."

Tell a golfer, "Don't hit that ball into the sand trap," and he or she will aim right for it. The body will follow the direction of the thought.

Thinking in terms of "don't" programs the mind to achieve a negative result. Unaware, we rehearse defeat by focusing on what we *don't* want instead of what we *do* want.

QLT *THEOREM*

FOCUSING ON WHAT YOU DON'T WANT IS JUST AS POWERFUL AS FOCUSING ON WHAT YOU DO WANT. BOTH CREATE RESULTS.

When you visualize a negative future, your body will react as if it were already true. If I imagine an audience responding negatively to my speech, I feel a tightening in my stomach. I remind myself to reframe my mental movie to see the response I want. I see and feel myself presenting my speech, I see and hear the audience responding enthusiastically, and I notice an immediate change in my physical state.

While race car training, we were told, "Always look where you want to go." At the firewalk, Bruce told us to see ourselves on the other side of the bed of hot coals. If you find yourself thinking about what you *don't* want to happen, consciously switch your picture to a positive outcome. Think about what you *do* want to happen or where you *do* want to end up. Think about what you *do* want to say, not about what you don't want to say. Think about how you *do* want to look, not how you don't want to look.

When Michelangelo was asked how he created his classic sculpture of David, he said that he took a large piece of marble, imagined the sculpture in vivid detail, and then chipped away everything that wasn't David.

That is how we create our lives. The *concept* has to appear in the imagination before we can manifest it into reality. The smoker must first see herself as a nonsmoker; the overweight man must first see himself with the weight off. Change follows image.

In my presentations I ask for examples of how members of the audience use visualization. Here are a few responses:

- Before giving a presentation, I rehearse the script of what I'm going to say and I imagine a positive audience reaction. It gives me self-confidence and has a positive effect on my behavior.
- I visualize to improve my skiing, bowling, golf game, or tennis game.
- When I imagine every possible objection my customer could have when I'm making a sales pitch, I go into the meeting with confidence, fully prepared to handle any obstacle.
- When I imagine communicating with my children with love, it affects the way I discipline them.
- I mentally rehearse job interviews. I see what I'm wearing. I see the office. I see myself in control.
- I visualize successful confrontations with my employees.
- I see and feel myself energetic, healthy, and excited about life.
- I use visualization during labor and childbirth.
- I close my eyes and imagine myself at my favorite vacation spot in order to relax.
- I'm a surgeon. I mentally run through a difficult surgical procedure to rehearse the options that may be necessary in case of complications.
- I visualize past successes. It not only gives me confidence in my present task, but I also feel motivated.

1. Be Clear About What You Want.

Write a list of everything you want to achieve. Review the list, and eliminate the ones that are not priorities. Eliminate goals that you chose because they're expected of you by someone else or are motivated by guilt. Repeat the process until you have one or two goals on which to focus. As your list grows smaller, you'll discover your remaining desires have grown more important.

2. Align Your Goals With Your Values.

Your goals must reflect what you value most. When what you think you want is in conflict with your values, the result is either self-defeating behavior or a feeling of emptiness if you finally succeed.

3. Put Yourself in a Receptive State.

Quiet your mind-chatter and open your subconscious to receive mental pictures. You are programming your brain-computer. Think of your conscious mind as a camera and your subconscious mind as the film. Relaxing the conscious mind is like pushing the shutter button. Images become imprinted on the film.

You may already have your own method of relaxing, but for those who have never consciously used a relaxation technique, here are a few suggestions:

Recall a place where you have felt at peace—maybe a vacation spot or a childhood playground. Shut your eyes and use your imagination. Pay attention to detail. Notice the colors, sounds, temperature, textures, smells, and emotions. You will find that with practice you can relax anytime, anyplace in a matter of seconds.

Another popular method of relaxing is "point-by-point" relaxation:

a. Find a quiet location, take the phone off the hook, and make sure you won't be disturbed.
b. Sit in a comfortable chair and dim the lights.
c. Close your eyes and become aware of the temperature of the room, the pressure of your body against the chair, your breathing, the beat of your heart, and your emotions.
d. Tense your body, then relax it, beginning with your face, moving to your shoulders, then your arms, hands, stomach, and legs.

e. Take three deep breaths. Inhale through your nose and exhale slowly through your mouth. Count to five on the inhale and to five on the exhale. After three slow, deep breaths, resume normal breathing.

You have now selected a goal aligned with your values and put yourself in a state of receptive relaxation. You are now ready to create your own personal feature film.

4. Make Your Visualization Real.

Experience it as if it were already happening. You want to see it, hear it, taste it, smell it, and feel it in the greatest detail possible. The words *visualization* and *mental imagery* can be frustrating if you believe that in order to be successful, you must actually *see* pictures.

Some people are more attuned to the auditory (hearing), kinesthetic (feeling), or olfactory (smelling) than the visual. One of my friends cannot actually see pictures and images, but she *feels* through her process. Whatever works for you is exactly the right method. If you can incorporate hearing, seeing, tasting, feeling, and smelling into your mental movie, do it. The more detailed you make it, the more real it is; the more real it is, the greater the power to imprint on your subconscious.

Let's pretend you have to present a speech at a meeting. Create the scene on a big screen. Create the room where you will give your speech. Fill in the details: the chairs; the stage, platform, or podium; the color of the walls; the size of the room; and the number of windows.

Add your audience. Are they dressed casually or in suits and ties? Hear the chatter as they settle down. Hear yourself being introduced. Hear the audience applaud. You are in perfect control. The audience quiets and gives you their attention. You are confident. You present your speech with enthusiasm. If there are jokes, hear laughs. Your colleagues are paying attention, and at the conclusion they applaud again. You feel wonderful.

Go through your speech again and again. Each time, add more details. Make the experience brighter, bigger, and clearer, using all your senses. The more vivid you create your experience, the more you will believe in it and the more successful you will be. Confidence creates magic.

5. Energize Your Visualization.

Give it as much high-powered emotion as you can. Recall a time when you were tremendously successful and carry that positive emotion into your present visualization. Excitement, love, confidence, curiosity, and enthusiasm all help eliminate negativity.

6. Visualize Often.

There is negative input all around us, from the time we wake up in the morning to the time we go to bed at night: grisly news reports, traffic, gossip, complaints, doubts, and worries. Negativity sticks like thistles, but positive visualization is a great remedy. It's like taking a mental bath to scrub away negative thoughts.

The more you visualize, the better you get at it. The clearer, more detailed, and consistent your visualization, the more likely you are to attract and notice opportunities to make your dream come true.

7. Visualize Before You Go to Sleep.

Positive visualization is a great way to prepare for a good night's sleep. You create a positive frame of mind before you end the day, and while your conscious mind sleeps, your subconscious is still on the job, awake and functioning. The subconscious takes what it was given, categorizes, organizes, files, and makes sense out of things. Feed the subconscious the material to work with just before you go to sleep, and you give it six to eight hours to work on your desired outcomes.

If you are impatient for results, add another visualization upon awakening. You will be surprised at the positive energy it gives to the beginning of your day.

8. Support Your Visualization With Affirmations.

You can use positive self-talk like "I deserve this" or "I am becoming what I want to be."

You can write your affirmations on paper and carry them with you, glancing at them whenever you choose. You can hang pictures on the wall to support your visualization or record a cassette tape and play it for yourself.

9. Trust and Be Patient.

Remember the process of baking bread? For true peace of mind while working on your goals, be patient. Commit to your daily routine, focus on your outcome often, affirm, and then let go, trust, and give the process time to work.

10. Be Grateful.

Make a list of your blessings. When you achieve your positive outcomes designed by the power of your positive visualization, be grateful and give thanks.

If I were in charge of the educational system, I would insist that every child be taught visualization. I would teach children to be aware of how they create their own futures and to assume responsibility for their own reality. I would teach them that with every choice we make, we give up some other possibility—and that we must be willing to pay the price. I would teach them accountability.

A large portion of my Positive Self-Image Training workshops was devoted to visualization. The participants were required to commit to using mental rehearsal for one full week to work on something they wanted, anything from losing weight to relationships, from developing self-confidence to creating a work of art. What surprised me most was not the results achieved; I knew most of the participants would be successful.

What surprised me was that some of the workshop attendees were actually afraid. The knowledge that the consciously controlled use of the imagination through visualization could create a result evoked fear of responsibility and accountability. Some participants simply did not want to acknowledge or experience their own power. Those who did went away with a skill that produced changes and success.

Once we push the gate of the mind slightly ajar and let the light stream in, the meaning of life becomes silently revealed to us. The gate may be open, for one minute or for one hour, but in that period we discover the secret and neither weary time nor bitter woe can tear that priceless knowledge away from us. . . . Those of us who have taken this peep through the door of our own being are dumbfounded. We draw back surprised at the inscrutable possibilities of the Overself. Man as a spiritual being possesses a capacity for wisdom which is infinite, a resource of happiness which is startling.

—PAUL BRUNTON,
The Secret Path

TURN FEAR INTO POWER

In my view . . . the central problem of human consciousness
depends on the ability to imagine.

—JACOB BRONOWSKI,
The Origins of Knowledge and Imagination

I magine the following science-fiction-like scenario: At your fin-
gertips, you have a virtual reality projector that allows you to
take your thoughts, project them outward into the world, and
then walk right into them like a living hologram.

Now imagine that, through some miscalculation on your part,
the thoughts you projected came from your worst fears, and you
didn't realize your mistake before you stepped into your hologram. You are now living your worst fears. Worse yet, you don't
realize what you did.

Certainly your intention wasn't to create a fear-based hologram, but no one had given you an instruction manual. If someone
had, you would have known to select your thoughts more carefully. You would have been very, very careful to choose only positive thoughts, and your hologram would have been a magical,
vibrant, positive reflection of your imagination.

Sound fantastic? It isn't. The description of this virtual reality projector is how our minds work. Reality begins with a thought.

When you acknowledge your fears, you begin to diminish their control over you. A true understanding of how fear works in combination with your imagination gives you the power to transform the most limiting of fears into positive power; it provides you with an owner's guide for the mind.

Fears do not exist in the world. You can't point your finger and say, "Jim, there's the fear of rejection running around," or, "Look, there's the fear of failure doing a handstand."

Instead, we project our fears into the world, act as if they were true, and make choices based on that reality. We create a self-fulfilling prophecy; fear-based thoughts transform into a fear-based reality.

▨ FEAR: THE GREAT TRICKSTER

> So let me assert my firm belief that the only thing we have to fear is fear itself—nameless, unreasoning, unjustified terror which paralyzes needed efforts to convert retreat into advance.
>
> —FRANKLIN D. ROOSEVELT,
> thirty-second president of the United States

Fear lies and manipulates. Fear inhibits us from facing challenges and taking risks. Fear clogs us with guilt, perpetuates the cycle of worry, and lets the imagination run wildly out of control. Fear distorts reality and focuses on imagined obstacles and problems. Many of us think that logic, willpower, or conscious reasoning can overcome fear. If only it were that simple.

◾ Q L T *THEOREM*

FEAR IS FALSE EVIDENCE APPEARING REAL.

Pretend, for the moment, that fear really doesn't exist, that it is an illusion—false evidence that appears real.

Pretend that, unconsciously, you seek out and accumulate the necessary facts or evidence to prove your fears to be true. Fear feels real and looks real, and you can back it up with evidence. You see what you believe, and what you see becomes proof. That is the elegance of your imagination, the source of power for the Great Trickster.

Q L T *THEOREM*

THE FIRST STEP TO TURN FEAR INTO POWER IS TO ACCEPT FULL RESPONSIBILITY FOR YOUR CHOICES, BEHAVIOR, AND THE REALITY OF WHAT YOU NOW HAVE IN YOUR LIFE. THE SECOND STEP IS TO HAVE THE COURAGE TO ACKNOWLEDGE AND EXAMINE YOUR FEARS.

All our fears grow out of a core fear of loss: loss of control, love, esteem, or health. I view the fear of loss as the center of a wheel to which are attached the spokes of secondary fears: change, rejection, success, failure, commitment, and poverty.

Fear has its place, and in the proper circumstances, fear may save our lives. Fear can be a great motivator. In the deepest recesses of our genes still lingers a very basic survival tool, the fight-or-flight syndrome. Many of us still unconsciously respond from that primitive mechanism that once served us so well. Lions and tigers and bears take on different personalities. We often interpret minor annoyances as threats to our basic survival and act accordingly.

Fear works in the most subtle ways. We can go through life never recognizing its presence, and few people realize how they are handicapped, physically and spiritually, by it.

Acknowledging our fears gives us the power to differentiate between reality and illusion, a difference that affects our life choices. We have a choice: We control the Trickster or the Trickster controls us. We operate the projector, and we can do it right.

Our most common fears are fear of rejection, change, success, failure, commitment, and poverty. These fears aren't necessarily destructive. Fear can be exciting, invigorating, and motivating.

The first and great commandment is: Don't let fear scare you.

—Anonymous

It is easy to confuse excitement with fear. Actors, athletes, artists, dancers, salespeople, and public speakers usually admit to having butterflies before they go onstage, or compete, or negotiate. Many of them say they would feel lost without that delicious tingle: It gives them energy and focus.

I have been appearing before some kind of audience since I was sixteen, and I can't remember when I didn't feel butterflies in my stomach before stepping onstage, but I have developed my own method of turning that sensation into excitement so that by the time I step out onto the platform, I am energized.

Ask yourself, "Is this fear really energy in disguise? Is it the old Trickster manipulating me into defeat? Or is it the invigorating, delicious side of fear waiting to encourage me?"

> A thousand fearful images and dire suggestions glance along the mind when it is moody and discontented with itself. Command them to stand and show themselves, and you presently assert the power of reason over imagination.
>
> —SIR WALTER SCOTT,
> Scottish novelist and poet

If we want to trick the Trickster, we have to examine the negative side of fear. Otherwise, we only justify our actions as we seek out the necessary evidence to support them. The choice to ignore the power of fear is the most frightening prospect of all.

Let's begin by examining the tools of the Trickster, those six fears. As you read through the descriptions, pay attention to your body; use the tool of truth. Ask yourself if you fall into any of these categories.

Q L T THEOREM

FEAR IN ITSELF IS NOT NEGATIVE; IT'S WHETHER YOU CONTROL THE FEAR OR THE FEAR CONTROLS YOU.

▇ THE SIX FACES OF FEAR

1. Fear of Change.

We talked about change in Chapter 4. Managing change is one of the three foundation skills of Quantum Leap Thinking. Change, you learned, is all about loss. Whether the change is for the better or not, we lose something in the process and we are thrust into the unknown.

2. Fear of Rejection.

I have never met anyone who is not afraid of rejection. It's normal. But the fear of rejection can trigger a self-protective mechanism that creates exactly what we dreaded: rejection. The Trickster's work is complete.

Fear of rejection can also manipulate us to be aggressive, controlling, possessive, or jealous. We tell ourselves that our behavior is justified. If we are aggressive and controlling, we can hold on to the people we love. The result, however, is that people feel trapped or intimidated. We push them away. We create rejection when what we want most is to be accepted. The need to control pushes away the very things desired: respect and compliance. We then blame others for not behaving the way we want them to. Or we blame ourselves.

Q L T *THEOREM*

FEAR DISTORTS OUR PERCEPTIONS AND MANIPULATES US TO CREATE WHAT WE FEAR MOST.

Do not remove a fly from your friend's forehead with a hatchet.
—Chinese proverb

If you are controlled by the fear of rejection, criticism can be perceived as just another form of rejection. Criticism is a sensitive issue even when our self-esteem is rock-solid. When we are weak, it can be deadly. It can manipulate us to wear certain clothes, drive a particular car, or go to what we think are all the right places—even if we don't really want to. When we are manipulated by fear of criticism, we sabotage our own integrity.

I will never forget, as a child, watching a friend's father strike him when he openly showed disagreement. It made me sick at heart.

The child who is criticized in an abusive manner grows into an adult who lacks self-esteem, and the abused child/adult continues being destructive; criticism then is almost always interpreted as rejection.

Unenlightened parents (or managers) become proficient at the art of using criticism to manipulate. They retard the creative spirit of the child or employee. On the other hand, constructive suggestion—criticism given with care and love—keeps the soul and spirit intact. Criticism then becomes a tool for learning instead of a weapon for destruction.

To give criticism with love and to receive criticism as feedback for learning is the mark of a Quantum Leap Thinker. The individual is not the outcome; you need to separate the person from what is being criticized. Maintaining someone's self-esteem is the number-one priority for empowerment.

My partner, Susan Granger, movie critic and corporate speaker, gives some wonderful advice on receiving criticism in her presentation "Don't Take It Personally: Conquering Criticism and Other Survival Skills." She says, "Don't be A.C.E.D. out by criticism."

A: Access the intention of the giver.
C: Consider the source.
E: Evaluate the nature of the criticism.
D: Delay reaction until your emotions are under control.

3. Fear of Success.

> The toughest thing about success is that you've got to keep on being a success. Talent is only a starting point in this business. You've got to keep on working that talent. Someday I'll reach for it and it won't be there.
>
> —IRVING BERLIN,
> American composer

I doubt that you have ever heard someone say he or she doesn't *want* to be successful, but we see people sabotaging their own success all the time.

Each of us has a unique picture of success. To some, success may mean having a certain position within an organization; to others, it may be measured by the amount of material possessions or money they've acquired. To the more enlightened, success may be having a loving family and friends.

Enter the Trickster. Fear can manipulate us to play it safe, resist taking risks, refuse to ask for what we want, be consistently late for appointments, insist on control, procrastinate, start projects but don't complete them, or choose inappropriate friends. Or simply to believe success is impossible.

"I will have too much responsibility."

"I would have to maintain it once I achieve it."

"People would expect too much of me."

"I would have to give up too much."

"My friends may no longer like me."

"People would be jealous."

The subconscious reads these thoughts as reality, and believe it or not, failure often creates a secret sense of relief. Fear of success must be acknowledged before it can be transformed into personal power.

Q LT *THEOREM*

SELF-SABOTAGE ENABLES AN INDIVIDUAL TO AVOID FACING IMPORTANT PERSONAL ISSUES.

4. Fear of Failure.

> Failure is, in a sense, the highway to success, inasmuch as every discovery of what is false leads us to seek earnestly after what is true.
>
> —JOHN KEATS,
> English poet

While working on the film *Star Trek VI: The Undiscovered Country,* I became friends with Roger, a middle-aged man who was working as an extra. It was obvious to me that Roger was well-read, highly intelligent, and compassionate, but he told me that he had worked at more than a hundred jobs in the previous five years. He had worked as a janitor at a fast food restaurant and a grocery packer at a food store. He had unloaded trucks and picked fruit. All the jobs he chose neither challenged nor inspired him. In other words, he chose jobs where he could not fail.

Roger had begun therapy a few months before I met him and had made great strides in discovering the source of his low self-esteem. What fascinated me was how his discovery had almost instantly changed how he viewed the world. He confided that his greatest insight occurred when he became aware that it was not others against him, as he had always believed, but his own lack of personal worth that had manipulated him to choose such menial jobs. He told me he no longer looked at himself as a victim and realized he was capable of much more than he had ever realized.

There are other tools the Trickster has at his disposal, like procrastination. It's an insidious, misguided perception that what needs to be done will be easier if we wait till tomorrow. Or maybe it won't have to be done at all! Procrastination is avoiding personal responsibility. Procrastination sucks the life out of our self-confidence, our creativity, ambition, and sense of possibility.

When we become aware of the reasons behind procrastination, we uncover the fear. We can then decide to move ahead. While the fear may not completely disappear, it no longer has a grip on us. Experience the fear and do it anyway.

Fear of failing can also persuade us to take poorly thought-out chances; our perception of risk becomes warped. Taking risks is no longer a tool for growth and learning; instead it manifests itself as foolish chances.

It's natural to fear failure when you start a new business, get promoted, begin a new relationship, prospect for new clients, ask for help, learn to ski, talk to an angry customer, present a new idea to the boss, or tell the truth. Be easy on yourself and others. Make fear your ally, your companion. Fear is a signal that you are stretching.

5. Fear of Poverty.

Real poverty exists in the world. Over 21 percent of children in the United States live in poverty, and we can't even begin to imagine the poverty in other countries. However, understanding how the fear of poverty gets in our way will make a profound difference in your attitude toward money, success, and prosperity.

Buried underneath the fear of poverty is the fear of death. Our very survival is threatened when we imagine not having enough to eat or a place to sleep. It touches our deepest, most primitive concerns. With most people, the denial of the fear of poverty is so complete and so unconscious that the fear can be as destructive as the reality.

> When you look at the world through the lens of scarcity, you will never have enough. When you view the world through the lens of abundance, you will always be wealthy.

Born in 1945, I am a product of Depression Era thinking. I remember when people still planted victory gardens and did without, just to get by. In reality, I never lacked for anything while I was growing up. Even so, my mother constantly worried about money. She worked part-time as a private nurse so she was able to give my brother and me allowances. She dragged us from grocery store to grocery store to save a few pennies on individual purchases. She was forever searching out sales. She hid emergency cash in the pages of books.

I remember her having arguments with my father; she criticized him for not pushing hard enough for a promotion or not asking for a raise. In truth, my father worked very hard at a job he didn't enjoy, and he did his best to provide for his family. He did not share the same fear of poverty as my mother, but her voice dominated the household.

This had a serious effect on me. I started working very young, but the fear of not having enough, which I unconsciously picked up from my mother, created years of anxiety and self-imposed stress. At the time I didn't know it.

My goal was to make money, and I was fortunate that I loved what I did. Nevertheless, my life was out of balance. The more I made, the less I felt I had. I increased my workload. If I was not actively earning money, I was either worrying about it or trying to come up with new ideas to earn even more. I'm sure the Trickster was grinning, because I was defeating myself even while earning more.

Sometime in the early 1980s I attended a lecture by Buckminster Fuller. His concluding words completely changed my definition of success. He said, "Riches are an accumulation of cash and things of no value to anyone. Wealth is freedom of mobility and freedom of choice. May you all be wealthy."

Right then I realized I had been allowing my fear of not having enough to destroy the enjoyment of what I had. I cringed at the unnecessary agony I had been putting myself through, and I began to recognize the fear at work in others.

When the fear of poverty is not acknowledged, we create our own poverty. We may choose to spend more than we make. We may work hard to earn more, but we spend more than we have again, as though we *liked* not having enough money.

Or we put everything we earn under the mattress, in the bank, or hidden between the pages of a book. Our car may be falling apart or our clothes in shreds, but we choose to save, save, save. The Trickster has done his magic. The prophecy is self-fulfilled; we feel poor.

6. Fear of Commitment.

> Always bear in mind that your own resolution to success is more important than one thing.
>
> —ABRAHAM LINCOLN,
> sixteenth president of the United States

Commitment is not to be taken lightly. Most people misunderstand the term or choose to conveniently redefine it. But there are no gray areas here. Commitment is not compliance. Commitment has nothing to do with convenience. Commitment simply *is*. Commitment is a way of being that defines your character.

> What you are thunders so that I cannot hear what you say to the contrary.
>
> —RALPH WALDO EMERSON,
> American poet and essayist

Top management consultant Kenneth Blanchard states, "There is a great difference between simple interest and commitment. When you are interested in doing something, you do it only when it's convenient. When you are committed to something, you accept no excuses, only results."

It is no wonder the Trickster is so powerful when fear of commitment enters the picture. The "what if's?" creep in, and decision making turns into fence sitting. What if I change my mind? What if I am trapped into doing something I don't want to do?

Those with the courage to commit are the ones with passion, energy, and enthusiasm. They have taken the stand to commit to something or someone.

E. Katherine Kerr, actress, playwright, teacher, and creator of *The Creative Explosion Workshop,* calls commitment the "I wanna's." In other words, you will commit only when, in the deepest part of you, you want to.

No one—no parent, teacher, government official, or manager—can make you commit to anything if you don't want to. You may go through the motions, but you will be operating out of compliance, not commitment. You will only commit because, for you, the payoff is greater than the sacrifice.

And sacrifice there will be. You can't manufacture more than twenty-four hours in a day, so you must carefully evaluate your reasons for making a commitment and verify to yourself that the commitment you make is aligned with your values and your needs.

Commitment gives strength, energy, and direction. Commitment allows you to manage change. Commitment doesn't suddenly, magically, appear, but the choice to commit can create seemingly magical outcomes.

Q LT *THEOREM*

COMMITMENT MAKES THE INVISIBLE VISIBLE.

Before I decided to buy my new Toyota Land Cruiser, I had never really noticed them on the road. The morning following my decision to buy one, I went out for breakfast to my local diner, and I could swear the world had just given birth to Land Cruisers. They were everywhere. Obviously they had always been there, but I hadn't noticed them because my mind-set made them, to me, invisible.

Commitment triggers a sort of inner picture. It provides you with an unconscious awareness of what you need or want. If it works for Toyota Land Cruisers, why can't it work for anything within the power of our imagination?

> Concerning all acts of initiative and creation, there is one ele-
> mentary truth, the ignorance of which kills ideas and splendid
> plans; that the moment one definitely commits oneself, then
> Providence moves too.
>
> All sorts of things occur to help one that would never have
> occurred. A whole stream of events issues from the decision,
> raising in one's favor all manner of unforeseen incidents and
> meetings and material assistance, which no man could have
> dreamt would have come his way.
>
> Whatever you can do, or dream you can, begin it. Boldness
> has genius, power and magic in it.
>
> —GOETHE,
> German poet and playwright

Recall the demonstration where I induced a hypnosis subject
to believe that the number eight did not exist. For all practical
purposes, the number became invisible. Think of the demonstration in reverse. In a way, through commitment, we can hypnotize—or dehypnotize—ourselves into seeing what we had not seen
before. We can make that number exist.

The term *synchronicity*, coined by psychologist Carl Jung,
provides an ideal platform for understanding the concept of
making the invisible visible. *Synchronicity* means "meaningful
coincidence."

You may wish to look at the phenomenon as extracting from the
universe what you need to support your commitment. Whatever
view you choose to take, the end result is the same. It works like
magic.

Henry David Thoreau said most men live lives of quiet desperation. We wish and fantasize and may even have good intentions,
but somehow we have not developed whatever it takes to make a
commitment. We are bored, we change our minds and complain,
we find excuses, and we drag ourselves out of bed to go to work.
Too many of us view ourselves as victims of our destiny.

Commit comes from the Latin *committere*, which means "to
ignite action, to bring together, join, entrust, and *do.*"

Commitment blossoms from our own desires. Commitment is
the *desire* and *willingness* to do whatever it takes to get what you
want. It is a promise of the heart from which you will move forward, no matter the resistance or barriers.

Commitment transforms fear into power, rendering the Trickster helpless. But commitment also creates change, and change creates resistance—from your boss, co-workers, friends, or family members. You may face what looks like impossible odds and a lack of support, resources, or funds. People may try to sabotage your efforts out of their own fears. You may have to battle bureaucracy. People might tell you that you're wrong, unrealistic, or just plain crazy. This means you're probably on the right track.

Don't take commitment lightly. Before committing to anything, you must carefully weigh the consequences of your decision. You must give up something to get something. I consider every important decision I make by visualizing a scale like the scales of justice with two trays hanging from a chain, perfectly balanced. On one side of the scale, I list the possible payoffs; on the other, the sacrifices or the price I must pay.

The uniqueness of your ideas and the power of possibility will generate resistance, but the power of your commitment will always pick you up if you're discouraged.

QLT *THEOREM*

FEAR NEVER WORKS AS A LONG-TERM MOTIVATIONAL TOOL AND WILL ALWAYS NEGATIVELY AFFECT THE QUALITY OF PERSONAL PERFORMANCE.

Dr. W. Edwards Deming, the guru of total quality, makes clear the necessity of eliminating fear in the workplace. The eighth of his fourteen-point quality system states, "Drive out fear, so that everyone may work effectively for the company."

Don't confuse pressure with fear. People perform well under pressure; they do not perform well when they are afraid. Problems turn into blame, and we attempt to defend ourselves. In the long term, motivation by fear backfires.

Fear may get short-term results, but fear prevents people from thinking clearly. It kills creativity and inspiration. Fear causes accidents, waste, and loss. We try too hard, take shortcuts, and hoard information. We don't trust people. We lie.

People who employ fear tactics believe that without threats, people won't perform; yet when threatened, they don't. The Trickster scores again.

Q L T *THEOREM* ─────────────────────────────

FEAR ITSELF IS NEVER THE PROBLEM. THE REAL PROBLEM
IS THE PERCEPTION OF FEAR.

Fear is a natural part of the growth process, so as long as you continue to grow, you will sometimes be afraid. Instead of using your energy to prevent fear, direct your energy where it will do some good.

Start with something small. Choose something you are afraid to do and do it anyway. With fear as your ally, you can take on bigger challenges. Fear becomes the signpost to move ahead instead of a signal to retreat.

Risking It All

Risk! Risk anything! Care no more for the opinion of others, for those voices. Do the hardest thing on earth for you. Act for yourself. Face the truth.

—KATHERINE MANSFIELD,
British short-story writer

There was that one brief moment when I felt my entire body go into frozen horror. I was staring down 13,000 feet, and then I was hurtling out into space. The leap may have been only two or three seconds, but in part of my brain I had experienced death.

I had toyed with the idea of skydiving for more than six years. I wanted to do a project on risk taking that would both teach the process of taking a risk and inspire people to take risks. I knew I would have to do something extraordinary, and whatever I chose must pit me against my own fear.

My inspiration came from the people who attended my seminars. I saw that most of them were reluctant to leave their personal comfort zone. They resisted taking risks.

But I learned something from them. Only about one out of

every ten said risk meant opportunity; to most it meant something dangerous, scary, or stupid. Yet the consensus was that most things worth having involved taking some kind of risk. It was an interesting paradox.

I figured that if I could demonstrate the nature of taking a risk, perhaps people could identify what risks they might take to enhance their lives and then develop a strategy for taking action. For the next four years I tried to promote the idea, hoping I could get outside financing for the project. There was mild interest, but no financial help.

I called a television producer friend of mine in Los Angeles and told her about the concept. She thought it was a terrific idea and agreed to check on costs and location. By the time she called me back, I had already decided to fund the project myself.

I had the first tingling of real fear on the flight to California. I have always been afraid of heights. I focused on rehearsing the script. I visualized speaking into the camera. I pictured myself being brave and vulnerable. The more I thought about it, the worse it got.

The day began early at a skydiving school. I met the crew and we set up for the straight camera shots. I was to jump in tandem with one of the instructors. We would free-fall 7,000 feet before the parachute opened. But first I had to sign my name to four pages of release forms and read a prepared statement into a video camera absolving the school of any responsibility should I be maimed or killed. My nerves gave a little warning tick.

We taped for five hours and took a lunch break. I watched ten jumpers, their parachutes explosions of color in the sky. It was beautiful. Some landed gracefully, and some did not. My knees began to ache.

Following lunch, the crew set up to record my twenty minutes of personal instruction. I put on a jumpsuit and a harness. I was instructed to watch the altimeter attached to my chest. When the needle reached 5,000, I was supposed to signal with a broad motion of my arms and pull the rip cord.

I felt something akin to excitement. Fear? I lay on my stomach in the grass with my arms spread wide, back arched and legs elevated, simulating the position I would assume in free fall. I decided it was definitely fear.

Instruction finished, the crew broke down the equipment and we began the trek to the plane. On the way I rehearsed the arm signal and the pulling of the rip cord.

Suddenly a police car raced out to the landing field. We all watched, and a fire engine joined the police car, followed by an ambulance.

I froze in my steps.

The instructor walked up to me and put his hand on my shoulder. "Don't worry," he said. "One of the school's cameramen landed wrong. He just hurt his leg. Nothing serious."

Why didn't that console me?

The camera crew recorded me boarding the plane, followed by a number of seasoned skydivers. Eight of us lined up in a tight row on the floor of the plane like dominoes. I leaned back, resting my tense body against the person behind me, and the person in front of me did the same. I was cramped and uncomfortable.

There were three camera operators on the plane with us. Two would jump with me, and the third would record my reactions as I left the plane.

The engines fired and we began to taxi down the runway. I felt extremely hot. One of the cameramen was perspiring so much he couldn't see through the lens. Watching him trying to wipe the perspiration out of his eyes while juggling his huge camera made me even more miserable. I felt sick to my stomach. A thought hit me like a thunderclap: *What if I chicken out at the last minute?*

"You're going to change your mind," said some unidentified voice in my head. "That's okay," my mother's voice said. "Better safe than sorry." I saw all that planning and money going down the drain.

We made one pass over the field. My instructor shouted at me that we would jump on the second pass. I watched as the first two jumpers saddled up to the open door. The noise was deafening.

The first skydiver disappeared just like a magic trick.

Pull yourself together, I thought to myself. Another one disappeared and another and another. The door closed.

"What are you feeling?" the cameraman asked.

I looked straight into the lens, searching frantically for an emotion. "Nothing."

"Three minutes. Let's buckle up." My instructor attached me

to his harness and repeated the instructions about the rip cord. The door opened again. Air rushing. I looked into the camera again, searching for some feeling, and found it: terror. I turned away from the unblinking eye of the lens. We duck-waddled on our knees to the door.

"On the count of three, lean out the door and fall forward," the instructor yelled over the sound of rushing wind. "One." He rocked me forward and backward. I felt faint. "Two." I started to hyperventilate. "Three." I fell forward into nothingness. I was convinced I had died.

After the first three or four seconds of feeling I had died, I realized that I was in free fall. I looked around. Unbelievable. The earth appeared as a quilt of brown patches. I looked at the altimeter: 9,000 feet. I looked out again. I was a sponge soaking in magic. The ground now appeared to be divided into symmetrical plots. I was flying. The camerawoman floated in front of me, smiling.

"This is great!" I yelled at the top of my lungs and gave her a thumbs-up sign. My voice was lost in the rushing of the wind. I reminded myself to check the altimeter: 6,000, 5,000. I gave the signal, reached blindly to my chest, and pulled the metal handle. We bounced up in the air.

The instructor screamed in my ear, "You did great! How do you feel?"

Joy swept through me like a flush of warmth. We floated down, playing with the controls of the parachute. Turning, spinning. I felt dizzy. "I don't want to do that," I yelled. "I don't want to spin."

We steered the chute straight ahead. Down below, I could see the camera crew running like a cluster of ants to the landing site. We closed in on the ground, pulling the handles of the chute just before we hit. I landed gently on my toes.

I couldn't believe it. I felt light-headed and shaky. The camera moved in on me. Bubbling up from some primitive place, I let out a triumphant cry of victory.

"How do you feel?" my instructor asked me again. Tears sprang to my eyes. I choked; I couldn't talk. I tried again. Nothing. I turned away from the camera, exposed and raw.

In retrospect, I realize that I accomplished everything I intended and more. I never really believed I would get so much out of the experience. My goal of making the documentary on risk taking was accomplished, but the experience had far exceeded my goal.

It doesn't matter how small or how great the risk may seem to others. The payoff, like mine, will more than likely exceed your greatest expectations.

> Take calculated risk. That is quite different from being rash.
> —GEORGE S. PATTON,
> American general

Saying "I love you," "I'm sorry," or "thank you," or giving someone a hug are risks. Telling the truth or saying no, changing jobs, starting a new business, getting married, or getting out of a relationship that doesn't work—those are risks, too.

Q LT THEOREM

SOMETIMES TAKING A RISK INVOLVES CHANGE. SOMETIMES TAKING A RISK MEANS COMMITTING TO REMAIN IN YOUR PRESENT CIRCUMSTANCE.

Risk taking is a subjective experience. One person's risk may be another's hobby. Sometimes risk is forced on you. Your mate of twenty years suddenly demands a divorce, or your job is terminated after thirty years. Imposed risks are often perceived as negative.

We would prefer to choose our risks. A chosen risk may be to tackle a new job or enter a new relationship, or opting to stay committed to a challenging job or relationship—a risk without major change.

It is vitally important to understand that how you perceive a risk, either imposed on you or chosen by you, can be the determining factor in whether it is an opportunity or a disappointment. By reframing your perspective of an imposed risk, you can turn it into an opportunity rather than a trap.

One thing is certain. Risk taking is the spice of life. Risk taking means growth and innovation. Taking risks is stretching to meet your potential.

To dare is to lose one's footing momentarily. To dare is to lose one's self.

—SOREN KIERKEGAARD,
Danish philosopher and theologian

Sir Laurence Olivier said that you could never be a great actor unless you were willing to make a total ass of yourself. The ultimate challenge is to risk the possibility of criticism. I put myself on the line to teach what I believe in, even if it does not match the opinions of the company who hired me. I have to. How could people believe me otherwise?

Risk takers are . . . extremely cautious people. An extraordinary amount of intelligence goes into preparing for their activities. They have analyzed every factor that can operate against them.

—DR. BRUCE OGILVIE,
sports psychologist

Here are seven steps to empower you to move beyond idea into action. While the steps to risk taking are similar to the steps for managing change, there are subtle differences.

1. Define What a Risk Is for You.

Before you rush out to skydive, change a relationship, or invest your money, take a moment to consider what taking a risk means to you. Your perception is your reality. No one else can define for you what you experience as dangerous. Give yourself credit for the smaller, demanding risks you have taken already and determine how any risk can enhance your life before jumping into a situation that may do more harm than good.

2. Imagine the Worst-Case Scenario.

This tip comes from NASA. Before taking a flight into space, astronauts are asked to imagine their worst fears. They repeat the process over and over. The more the astronaut imagines the worst, the more he or she desensitizes his or her mind. Astronauts who are not able to accept the worst-case scenario are not allowed to go into space.

By consciously asking yourself or others what's the worst that can happen, you perform a reality check. Often the imagination will conjure up something far worse than reality.

3. Seek as Much Information About the Risk as Possible.

Risk takers prepare. They play out every possible outcome. They do their homework. The more you know about the risk, the better you can prepare. The more you prepare, the more confident you become. The more facts you have, the less chance for failure.

4. Talk to Others.

Ask people whose opinions you trust. Open yourself up to feedback, but be cautious. We all have a tendency to advise others about what to do and what not to do. Don't let yourself be manipulated. The purpose of feedback is to allow you to see as many different points of view as possible before you make your own decision.

5. Create a Safety Net.

A safety net is anything that keeps you from feeling your choice is irreversible. Plan options to cover yourself if your risk does not work. You may wish to take a leave of absence as opposed to quitting your job, or you may arrange a trial separation instead of getting divorced.

6. Reframe the Outcome.

You can take one small step at a time; you don't have to do it all at once. Focusing on the end result can increase the fear and cut off action.

This was evident to me when I started skiing. I got my ski legs on the beginner's slope and then took a lift to one of the more advanced runs. I shuffled to the edge of the run and looked down to the bottom of what looked like the steepest mountain in the world. I panicked, took off my skis, and stumbled all the way down.

An instructor suggested we go back to the top, where he had me take one simple turn and stop. He then asked me to do another. And another and another. I gradually reached the bottom. We went back and did it again. That time I stopped only three times, and on the next run only once. By changing my focus, I changed my performance.

7. Seek Support.

Find people who have beliefs similar to yours. Seek out those who will hold you up when you need courage, people who genuinely care about your efforts, your growth, and your happiness. Support encourages you to live up to your highest potential.

> You gain strength, courage, and confidence by every experience in which you really stop to look fear in the face. You are able to say to yourself, "I have lived through this horror. I can take the next thing that comes along." You must do the thing you think you cannot do.
> —ELEANOR ROOSEVELT

I believe we are born risk takers. Think about it. How did you learn to walk or to ride a bike? We learned more and faster in the first five years of our lives because we had not yet been taught fear. The word *impossible* did not yet exist. We made mistake after mistake, shook them off, and gave it another try. Watch children to learn about taking risks.

Not taking risks is far more dangerous than taking them. Not taking risks accelerates the aging process. We feel helpless and hopeless, trapped in a world without choices. You can see it in the body and feel it in the soul.

But our lives can be daring adventures if we understand how to orchestrate risk taking, to articulate adventure. Adventure creates relationships and relationships give life meaning. Risk taking promotes vibrancy, energy, and good health. You learn and you grow. Your days become more rewarding, vital, and fulfilled. In your own way, you walk on fire.

RISKING

To laugh is to risk appearing the fool.

To weep is to risk appearing sentimental.

To reach out for another is to risk involvement.

To expose your feelings is to risk exposing your true self.

To place your ideas and your dreams before a crowd is to risk embarrassment.

To love is to risk not being loved in return.

To live is to risk dying.

To hope is to risk despair.

To try is to risk failure.

But risks must be taken, because the greatest hazard in life is to risk nothing at all.

The person who risks nothing does nothing, has nothing, and is nothing.

They may avoid suffering and sorrow, but they cannot learn, feel, change, grow, love or live.

Chained by their certitudes, they are slaves. They have forfeited their freedom.

Only a person who risks is free.

—Love Unlimited

BALANCING
YOUR LIFE

STRATEGIES FOR BALANCE

There are two things to aim at in life: first, to get what you want; and after that to enjoy it. Only the wisest of people achieve the second.

—LOGAN P. SMITH,
American writer

A few years ago I was invited to attend a men's retreat in Colorado. Counting myself, our group consisted of ten men. The other nine were either presidents of large corporations or owners of successful businesses, all extremely wealthy. The majority were middle-aged, married with grown children, and had never attended an event of this type.

I had no idea what to expect. My sole preparation was to read two books on the men's movement. I found the information mildly interesting, but in my opinion a little strange.

The retreat was a real eye-opener. The two-and-a-half days were devoted to open, vulnerable self-exploration. We wrestled with concepts like finding balance in our lives and discovering purpose. What impressed me most was the willingness of the men to explore their own thoughts and suspend judgment of others. And there were a lot of tears shed.

These men had achieved what they had thought was success, but they felt a deep disappointment. More than a few expressed profound sorrow at having missed their children's development while in pursuit of what they now viewed as an illusion.

There are many men and women who have come to the same point in their lives. They have discovered their personal road maps were faulty and their ultimate successes left them feeling needy.

We are constantly bombarded by other people's definitions of success. Whether we realize it or not, we are being manipulated. We have to remember that when we are not living according to our values, we develop an internal hunger. You must consistently ask yourself if you are staying true to what you value.

The definition of success is slippery, shifting with age, experience, and achievement. Most of us work hard and make sacrifices to buy a house or a second car, and the irony is that with the accumulation of all these new things comes a whole new set of responsibilities that restrict our freedom and often pressure us to work even harder. We may live in constant fear that someone or something will take away what we have worked so hard to attain.

Is this a life of quality? Is this what our journey to mastery is all about?

Back in 1970 psychologist Abraham Maslow, in his book *Motivation and Personality*, created a hierarchy of human needs. He said that the lowest level of needs, our basic needs (air, food, shelter), must be met to some degree before we can move forward to our wants. The satisfaction of the next level, our *wants*, has a direct effect on our health and may even contribute to longevity.

The highest level in Maslow's hierarchy is companionship and affection. Love is a necessity for continued good health and growth. We must feel that someone cares, that we have personal worth. Praise, reward, or recognition is of vital importance in both the family and the organization. Remove love, real or imagined, and our self-image falls into a black hole.

> Even if all these needs are satisfied, we may still often expect that a new discontent and restlessness will soon develop unless the individual is doing what he is fitted for. A musician must make music, an artist must paint, a poet must write if he is to

be ultimately at peace with himself. What a man can be, he must be. This need we call self-actualization. —ABRAHAM MASLOW

Q L T *THEOREM*

SUCCESS IS USING EVERYTHING YOU HAVE TO BE AND DO EVERY-THING YOU ARE CAPABLE OF WITHIN THE ARENA YOU HAVE CHOSEN.

I have noticed a major shift from the attitude of "me-me" and "more-more" to a yearning for something greater than money and material possessions. People seem to be searching for balance in their lives and a higher purpose. I see it with employees of major insurance companies, computer corporations, health-care specialists, and even concrete makers. In fact, during every presentation I make, I sense this need, perhaps not by everyone, but certainly by the majority. People are hungry for knowledge about values and vision. They are searching for meaning.

This is not accidental. I believe we have actually learned something from the excesses of the eighties. We are feeling the pain that signals the need for change.

Many of us get trapped in Maslow's first stage of the hierarchy, and we still feel we don't have enough. Perhaps it is a reflection of societal manipulation, or perhaps it is as simple as not being aware that, at our deepest level, we are safe and secure.

Whatever the reason, many of us tend to focus our life's energies on our jobs at the expense of our families, our health, fun, and spirituality. By seeking fulfillment and rewards in our careers, we tend to neglect other areas. The struggle becomes the norm and, being familiar, goes unrecognized.

You never conquer the mountain; you only conquer yourself.
—JIM WALKER,
who climbed Mount Everest

Ben Franklin in Paris, by Sidney Michaels, is one of my favorite American musicals. In it, Ben Franklin sings a song called "I Invented Myself." We do invent ourselves. We invent ourselves by choosing to live the way we live. For me, the magic of the song on a much deeper level, however, is that we have the power to continuously reinvent and renew ourselves.

How would you act if your actions truly flowed from your values? If you act as though they do, your actions will create new habits and ultimately change how you think. Attitude does not necessarily alter behavior, but behavior does affect attitude.

> Harmony: the pleasing combination of tones in a chord.
> —*Webster's New World Dictionary*

Harmony is the closest word I can find to express my feelings about balance. When the areas of your life are in balance, you resonate; you are in tune. Evaluate your life as a system and develop a holistic approach to living. When the parts of your life are balanced, quantum leaps take place naturally and effortlessly.

> Creatively successful people make a point of noticing when their lives go out of balance.
> —MICHAEL RAY AND ROCHELLE MYERS,
> *Creativity in Business*

How balanced is your life? Below are seven categories of needs vital to a life of balance and harmony. Consider carefully how much energy and time you spend on these different aspects of your life. Then take a piece of paper or your journal and give each category a rating from one (very little time and energy) to ten (much time and energy). You may find that some categories overlap. Don't worry about it.

- Emotional well-being
- Spirituality
- Career
- Relationships
- Mental stimulation
- Physical health
- Financial security

When you put too much energy in one area at the expense of another, you will find your life out of sync. You may need to reevaluate where and how you focus your energy.

Once you decide where to refocus your energies, read ahead and find the appropriate section. You will find some suggestions on how to direct your focus to put more harmony in your life.

▮ QUANTUM LEAP STRATEGIES FOR EMOTIONAL WELL-BEING

Cherish your own emotions and never undervalue them.
—ROBERT HENRI,
American painter

1. Challenge your beliefs about the way things should be. If you think the problem is "out there," your thinking is the problem. Discover your outdated beliefs that are the cause of your emotional turmoil and change them.
2. Give yourself permission to experience the emotions you're feeling. It is only when you can acknowledge your emotions that you can deal with them in a proactive manner.
3. Understand that the emotions you feel are not caused by people or situations; emotions are your reactions to people and situations. Negative, fear-based emotions, such as hostility, anger, anxiety, and insecurity, are caused by your *responses* to circumstances, not by the circumstances themselves.

Dr. Maxwell Maltz, author of *Psycho-Cybernetics*, uses the metaphor of tranquilizers to draw an ideal analogy. He writes:

Tranquilizer drugs . . . bring peace of mind, calmness, and reduce or eliminate nervous symptoms by an umbrella action. Just as an umbrella protects us from the rain, the various tranquilizers erect a psychic screen between us and disturbing stimuli. . . . Tranquilizers work because they greatly reduce, or eliminate, our own response to disturbing stimuli. . . . Tranquilizers *do not change the environment*. The disturbing stimuli are still there. We are still able to *recognize* them intellectually, but we do not *respond* to them emotionally. . . . As with happiness, our own feelings do not depend on externals, but upon our own attitudes, reactions and responses. . . . Tranquilizers reduce or tone down our over-response to negative feedback.

Q L T *THEOREM*

OUTSIDE STIMULI OR SIGNALS, IN AND OF THEMSELVES, HOLD NO POWER OVER YOU. YOU GIVE OR TAKE AWAY THE POWER OF OUT-SIDE STIMULI BY HOW YOU CHOOSE TO RESPOND TO THEM.

In much the same way that a burglar alarm is programmed to respond to physical movement, you have been programmed to respond to outside stimuli. Because you have the power to repro-gram yourself, you can, if you wish, become your own tranquilizer.

Pavlov conditioned dogs to salivate at the sound of a bell by ringing it just prior to mealtime. He repeated the process over and over, until the dog eventually learned to salivate in anticipa-tion of food. The surprise came when the dog salivated whenever the bell was rung, even when food was not forthcoming. The dog was now programmed, or "conditioned." A habit was formed, and even though the animal's response made no sense and served no purpose, the habit continued.

We all have "bells." Some of our emotional habits are relatively harmless and some serve a good purpose, but others create stress.

4. Your emotions are real. They are part of the process of living and must be respected and honored. That means they need to be expressed. When you feel joy, express it with delight. When you feel sad, cry. When you're angry, give yourself permission to yell. However . . .

5. Find creative ways to express your feelings, ways that are not harmful to others or to yourself. When you're angry, count to ten. It's hard to retract what you have said in anger, so find a healthier alternative. Yell at a tree; yell when you're alone; take your anger out in the gym; beat up a pillow. Han-dle your anger responsibly.

6. Be aware of your "hot button." Your hot button is like the trigger on a gun. When it's pushed, you respond instantly with irritation, anger, or sadness. It can be pushed by any-

one—your child, spouse, employee, or boss. Your hot button can be so emotionally powerful that you will respond without logic.

Use your reaction as a direction finder and discover the underlying belief that created the trigger. Ask yourself under what previous circumstances did you remember feeling the same way? You may recall a specific childhood circumstance and see a pattern.

For example, my hot button is pushed when someone orders me to do something. That probably stems back to suppressed anger toward authority figures when I was a child, and I still feel a slight tingle when I'm told to do something in a particular tone of voice. I take a deep breath and count slowly to ten. This gives me just enough time to realize that my anger has nothing to do with the person who gave me the order. I shift gears and consciously respond appropriately.

7. Let go.

> Therapeutic forgiveness cuts out, eradicates, cancels, makes the wrong as if it has never been. Therapeutic forgiveness is like surgery.
>
> —DR. MAXWELL MALTZ,
> *Psycho-Cybernetics*

Most of us carry an incredible amount of emotional baggage from the past: failure to reach our goals, failed relationships, infidelity, out-of-date beliefs of all kinds. The reasons for holding on to old resentments fill novels.

We are born with 100 percent of our creative potential. If 10 percent, 40 percent, or 80 percent of our creative energy is taken up with baggage, we are using up energy that could be put to better use.

Q L T *THEOREM*

LETTING GO IS A CHOICE.

A man is walking along the edge of a cliff. He stumbles and falls, tumbling into nothingness. In a panic, he reaches out and grabs a branch. Holding on with all his strength, he looks around. There are no other branches, nor is there a ledge on which to secure a leghold. Realizing he is about to die, he begins to pray in earnest.

"Please, God, are you there?"

A loud voice booms from the heavens. "You called?"

"Oh, yes," shouts the man. "God, is that really you?"

"Yes," God replies. "It's really me. What do you want?"

"Please, please save me! I will do anything you ask if you just save me! I beg you!"

"Anything?" God asks. "Really?"

"Oh, really, really! Anything!" the man yells.

God's voice is sure and strong. "Let go of that branch."

Looking up to the heavens in bewilderment, the man cries, "Are you crazy?"

L E T

G

O

What you are challenged to let go of is often the very thing that defines who and what you are: your ego. Or perhaps your present level of discomfort has become so familiar that it is more comfortable than the unknown. You can become so used to pain that the thought of letting go of it seems worse than the pain itself.

▞ A FOUR-STEP PROCESS FOR EMOTIONAL FREEDOM

> The truest joys they seldom prove,
> Who free from quarrels live:
> 'Tis the most tender part of love,
> Each other to forgive.
> —JOHN SHEFFIELD,
> poet and duke of Buckingham/Normandy

1. Identify Your Baggage.

Make a list of your hurts and resentments, including those caused by past lovers, family, co-workers, business associates, and childhood friends. Write them down in your journal or notebook.

2. Visualize the Source.

Close your eyes and imagine the person you hold the most anger and resentment toward sitting across from you. Tell her or him why you felt hurt. Be honest and express everything you feel needs to be said, everything that has been held back. Ask questions.

3. Hear the Explanation.

Listen to what the person says. Allow yourself to hear the full truth of what he or she tells you. Stop for a moment and notice if you have left anything unsaid. If so, express it and once again fully listen to his or her response.

4. Let Go.

Gently release the weight of your resentment toward the other person or toward yourself. In whatever way feels right to you, release the negative emotional energy that has, up to this point, been stuck. As you let go and release your anger, bitterness, or guilt, notice how you begin to lighten up. Take a deep breath and fully experience the release. You have experienced the magic of forgiveness.

You can use the same exercise to experience self-forgiveness. The more you use it, the lighter and clearer you will feel. The results are magical.

▓ QUANTUM LEAP STRATEGIES FOR MENTAL STIMULATION

> It is not enough to have a good mind; the main thing
> is to use it well.
> —RENÉ DESCARTES

1. Vary Your Mental Routine.

I've watched serious weight lifters work the hardest on the part of their body that is the easiest to develop. Or they work on their chest and ignore their legs. Some work out only with weights and ignore their cardiovascular system.

We have a tendency to do the same thing with our minds, but keeping the mind in shape demands a variety of exercises and experiences. My seventy-eight-year-old aunt does crossword puzzles. She knows it is vital to give her mind a workout. We need to maintain a deep sense of curiosity and, like the bodybuilders, we need to vary our routine.

> Men seek retreats for themselves: houses in the country, seashore and mountains; and thou too art wont to desire such things very much. . . . But this is altogether a mark of the most common sort of men, for it is in thy power whenever thou shalt choose to retire into thyself. For nowhere, either with more quiet or more freedom from trouble, does a man retire than into his own soul, particularly when he has within him such thoughts that by looking into them he is immediately in perfect tranquility. This is nothing else than the good ordering of the mind. Constantly then give to thyself this retreat, and renew thyself. . . .
>
> —MARCUS AURELIUS ANTONINUS
> Roman Emperor

2. Create a Mental Decompression Chamber.

I got hooked on scuba diving in the mid-seventies and have been an avid diver ever since. The first rule of diving always makes me smile: Keep breathing and relax. That makes diving seem pretty simple.

Diving *is* easy, but there are some very serious dangers if you don't relax. One danger is coming up to the surface too rapidly. The results can be disastrous. You can get too much nitrogen in your blood; it's unbearably painful and can end your diving career forever. Divers call this "getting bent." "Bent" divers are put in a decompression chamber to bring their blood oxygen level back to normal. Too much nitrogen in your blood will kill you.

I refer to the process of becoming relaxed as mental decompression. There is a place within you where nothing can disturb you, a place in the very center of you where you can decompress from the frustrations of life. This special place is built with the power of your imagination when you learn to quiet your mind. Going to your center allows you to decompress from everyday worries, stress, and tension.

I learned a wonderful visualization process. I imagine that I walk down a flight of ten stairs, take a special key out of my pocket, and open the lock on a thick steel door.

When I walk in, the lights go on. The room is big enough for me to feel a sense of openness. It is totally soundproof. It contains a bed, a large overstuffed easy chair, and an extra chair should I choose to invite a guest. On one wall hangs pictures of my loved ones. On another is a large bookshelf filled with some very special books and a large notebook I call my Journal of Life.

A small movie screen is set in one wall where I can project people, places, or images appropriate to my needs, complete with the music of my choice. I can walk into the picture on the screen, if I want to, and become part of a living hologram.

When I enter my room, I leave everything outside. There is no tension, no stress. I can direct everything that happens. I can sit in my chair and meditate. Sometimes I invite my grandfather for a visit. He is my counselor, and whenever I have a problem, he is there to give me advice. This is my idea of a perfect decompression chamber.

Dr. Maxwell Maltz writes, "Your soul and your nervous system need a room for rest, recuperation, and protection every bit as much as your physical body needs a physical house, and for the same reasons."

The beauty of a mental decompression chamber is that you can go there anytime you choose to recharge. And you can do it anywhere. You can go to your decompression chamber while in your own home, on a park bench, behind your desk, on the train to work, on a plane, or while the baby is sleeping. It is an invaluable mental tool.

3. Commit to Ongoing Learning.

There is a myth that learning is for young people. But it's what you learn after you know it all that counts. The middle and later years of life are great, great learning years.

Continuous learning is one of the three bases that form the foundation of Quantum Leap Thinking. Learning gives you balance in your life and leverage in the world of business. There was a time when "doing" was enough, but thinking makes you invaluable in today's marketplace.

Q LT *THEOREM*

YOU LEARN FROM EVERY EXPERIENCE YOU HAVE, EVEN IF IT DOESN'T SEEM LOGICAL.

True learning goes far beyond acquiring information and skills. As you mature, you learn not to waste precious energy on anxiety and fear. You learn not to engage in self-destructive behavior. You learn to associate with people who have a positive outlook on life. You learn how to manage tension. You learn that self-pity, resentment, jealousy, hate, anger, and envy are toxic emotional drugs. You learn that talent is wonderful, but life generally pays off on character.

I have been told that the majority of people are neither for nor against you; instead, they are merely thinking about themselves. You learn that when you smile most of the world smiles with you. You learn that no matter how hard you try to please, some people are not going to love you. You learn to find inner peace.

Take up a creative hobby. Learn basic Neuro-Linguistic Programming techniques. NLP gives you great tools to stretch your mental processes. Play games that require you to think. Choose to associate with stimulating people who bring new ideas to your mental table. Do something unusual that breaks your normal routine. Write letters, thank-you notes, poems, and stories. Keep a journal. Read. Read about science, philosophy, and other cultures. Read fiction, too; you want to stretch and work that mental muscle, not exhaust it. This book was a good place to start.

QUANTUM LEAP STRATEGIES FOR SPIRITUALITY

Be sure that it is not you that is mortal, but only your body. For that man whom your outward form reveals is not yourself; the

spirit is the true self, not that physical figure which can be
pointed out by your finger.
                                            —CICERO,
                                Roman statesman, orator, and author

Spirituality holds different meanings for different people. It is
highly personal and intimate. Spirituality should not be confused
with dogma or religion. It has nothing to do with the theological
definitions of what's right and wrong. Other people's concepts
about God have nothing to do with discovering, developing, and
nurturing what fulfills the deepest part of you.

I have asked many people what being spiritual means to them.
Their answers vary from the obvious to the surprising:

- Being connected to the earth.
- Being aware that I am part of a universal order.
- Contemplation; meditation; being in touch with my "higher
  self."
- Nature.
- Being a member of a church and participating in church
  functions.
- Helping others.
- The spiritual connection or wholeness after making love.
- Being in touch with and guided by my inner intuitive voice.
- Believing in God.
- Seeing myself as part of God.
- Loving myself and others.

The corporate world is slowly acknowledging the importance of
spiritual values. Matsushita employees, for example, refer to the
values of harmony and cooperation, struggle for betterment, fairness, gratitude, and courtesy and humility in their company litera-
ture. Many of the corporate vision statements handed to me over
the past few years include "respecting the dignity of the individual," "telling the truth," and "becoming responsible members of
the community."

The way you choose to achieve balance in your spiritual life
isn't important. What matters is the balance itself. When you view
your life as having a higher purpose, you tap into an extraordinary
inner resource of motivation. Gandhi called it *satyagraha,* or "soul

force." You tap into love for yourself and others, along with creativity, communication with respect for the individual, cooperation, interdependence, trust in your higher self, and intuition.

Here is an exercise for getting in touch with the spiritual side of your nature.

1. Find a quiet place where you will not be disturbed. Close your eyes, take several deep breaths, and use your favorite relaxation process.
2. Create in your mind a relaxing place. Paint the picture; create a mental movie in detail, including smells, temperature, colors. The purpose of your journey is to meet the wisest being in the universe and to ask one question: What is my higher purpose, and how may I manifest it more fully in my life?
3. You see a light in the distance and, as you move closer, the form of that wisest being begins to take shape. You move closer still. The image sharpens. What do you see? Is this being in the form of an animal or a human, or is it a light? The being radiates peace and love. You approach the being without fear. It seems to await your question, and you ask it.
4. Allow the being to answer your question. The answer may come to you in the form of an emotion, another question, or a symbol. Or the answer may be directly to the point. Spend time contemplating whatever answer you receive. Be aware of your body. If the answer isn't clear, ask for clarity.
5. When you feel ready, open your eyes and write down your impressions of the wisest being. Draw a picture or write down and expand on the answer you received.

This visualization exercise has helped many people discover their higher purpose. You may already know what yours is. If so, use the exercise to validate it or simply to practice visualizing and trusting your intuition.

There are many ways to nourish your spiritual needs:

- Go to a house of worship.
- Plant a garden.
- Pray.

- Walk in the woods; connect with nature.
- Meditate.
- Exercise.
- Read inspirational books.
- Listen to inspirational tapes.
- Visit a home for senior citizens.
- Visit with terminally ill people.
- Listen to music that touches your spiritual side.
- Connect with other spiritual individuals.
- Sit quietly on a park bench.
- Walk on a beach.

Make spirituality a daily process of renewal in whatever way makes you feel comfortable. Stay in touch with your inner self, with your higher self, with your God-like self or soul, or with God or a higher being. It is not just a renewal process; it is a healing process.

QUANTUM LEAP STRATEGIES FOR PHYSICAL HEALTH

I recently spoke to a group of veteran's hospital administrators. The majority were in wheelchairs; some had artificial limbs, and some lacked both arms and both legs. But they were upbeat, curious, and obviously in control. Whatever process they went through to accept and deal with their physical challenges had been handled.

I wanted to ask them how they felt, how they had learned to cope. It took me a full two hours to work up the courage. I was afraid that my questions would offend them, but they weren't insulted.

They told me they didn't just cope. They had, through their spiritual growth and tenacity, become powerfully independent. They went through their own private hell and came out stronger. Furthermore, they had chosen to devote their lives to helping others with similar challenges.

Why focus on this group? Because of the number of people who are totally unconscious about their bodies. Because I have been one of those people who have everything intact yet still feel help-less and hopeless about their ability to change.

My motivation to get in shape was not as pure as I would have liked it to be. An aspiring actor, I wanted to project a particular image, and to do so, I had to get in shape and stay that way. It wasn't fun, and it didn't make me happy, but I worked out reli-giously every day.

I know something now that I didn't know then. I had ignored the other parts of my life while I focused on shaping up. I now know that my physical needs must be balanced with my other needs in order for me to be content.

If you rated yourself low in the physical needs department, you must do a major paradigm shift to focus on your relationship with your body. This has nothing whatsoever to do with how someone else may want you to look, nor is it about comparing yourself to others. It is not about guilt (reactive); it is about self-creation (proactive). It is about developing a consciousness and a connec-tion with your body. You become the designer, the creator, and once you make the commitment, you will be surprised at how quickly your physical self will respond.

Write the answers to these questions in your journal or note-book. Take your time with them. Draw pictures if it's easier.

1. What images come to mind when you think about your body?
2. How well do you take care of your body?
3. What food do you put in your body?
4. What kind of physical exercise do you give your body?
5. What is your vision for your body?
6. How do you want your body to feel?
7. How do you want your body to perform?

As you write, you will begin to develop a connection with your body. Like a complex machine, your body needs maintenance. Since creation always begins with questions, here are a few more for you to contemplate.

1. How do you feel about your overall energy, stamina, and endurance?
2. How do you feel about your overall physical condition?

3. Do you feel that your heart and cardiovascular system are healthy?
4. Do you feel flexible?
5. How do you feel about the foods you put in your body?
6. Do you get the amount of rest you need?
7. Take your clothes off and stand in front of a mirror. Do you have good muscle tone and strength?
8. Do you feel loved, appreciated, and cared for?

Q L T *THEOREM*

YOUR BODY IS A DIRECT REFLECTION OF YOUR BELIEFS.

You need to have an idea of what you want your body to be, but be realistic. For example, no matter how hard I work out or what I eat, I will never have a body like Arnold Schwarzenegger. I have more of a dancer's bone structure than a bodybuilder's. However, I do have some choices. I have control over my strength and flexibility and my cardiovascular health. Consult your physician, have a complete physical, and be realistic about your body before you tackle any strategies about designing a "new you."

Visualization is a tool with which you can transform your self-image and your physical being. Implant a new, ideal yet realistic image of yourself in your subconscious and you will move in the direction of your new vision.

VISUALIZE YOUR IDEAL SELF

1. Close your eyes, relax, and imagine yourself sitting in a chair. Ten feet to your left is a large mirror. An identical mirror is ten feet to your right.
2. Look in the mirror on your left and imagine you see yourself at your physical worst. Experience all the negative feelings you have ever had about your body and think all the negative thoughts you have ever thought about what you look like. Say them out loud.
3. Now look at the mirror on your right. Picture yourself exactly as you would *like* to look, as if the transformation had

already taken place. See yourself wearing the clothes that would show off your new physique. Feel the positive emotions and experience pride as you see your reflection. You are looking at your ideal self.

4. Look back at the mirror on the left. Once again feel your negative judgments. Now look under your chair and imagine a hammer there. Pick it up and either throw it at the mirror on the left and shatter it, or get up from your chair and smash the mirror into pieces.

5. Sit back in your chair and look at the positive mirror on your right again. This is a magical mirror. You can walk right into it and into your new body. Feel your new healthy self. Feel your muscle tone. Look at your arms and legs. Notice the flatness of your stomach. Relish the vitality. Bend over and touch your toes. Bend side to side. Experience your body's flexibility. Turn around. Stand on one foot, perfectly balanced. Feel your body's grace. Imagine yourself running. Test your stamina and endurance. You have achieved your optimal physical self.

Remember, reality happens twice: first in your mind, then in the creation.

I have not suggested dieting. Dieting is an example of negative programming. Most dieters place imagination in competition with willpower, consciously or unconsciously telling themselves that they are unattractive. When they stop dieting, they return to the image they hold of themselves. The imagination always triumphs.

Diets don't work in the long run, but developing a clear image of your ideal self and developing an action plan does. Change your attitude by changing your behavior.

The Magic of Exercise

After age twenty-five, we lose approximately one-half pound of muscle mass each year, but you don't have to be a statistic. Even people over seventy can change their physical structure. The body responds very quickly.

Conditioning has very little to do with age unless you believe age is limiting. There are people in their early forties who look sixty, and there are people in their seventies who have the vitality of people in their thirties.

Be gentle with yourself when you exercise. You want to build up gradually without straining muscles or hurting yourself. Take your time and be consistent. You *know* that exercise is good, but logic doesn't necessarily motivate you, does it?

> Better to hunt in fields for health unbought
> than see the doctor for a nauseous draught.
> The wise for cure on exercise depend
> God never made his work for man to mend.
> —JOHN DRYDEN,
> English poet

A study at the University of San Francisco's Human Performance Laboratory found that physically fit people have more control over their reactions to stress than those who are not fit. Consistent exercise is an invisible stress shield.

Exercise makes a major difference in attitude, energy, and performance. Exercise triggers the release of endorphins, the body's natural opiate and mood elevator. Exercise boosts your confidence. Exercise reduces jet lag. It's a necessity for me when I'm on the road. Exercise may well improve longevity and sexual drive as well as reduce the risk of heart disease.

Exercise clarifies your thinking. Erik Olesen writes in *Twelve Steps to Mastering the Winds of Change* that researchers at Scripps College studied a group of adults ages fifty-five to ninety-one, testing their memory, reaction time, and reasoning abilities. The physically fit men and women performed significantly better than those who didn't exercise.

I have questioned literally hundreds of people about why they exercise, and the response has invariably been, "It makes me feel good about myself." And when you feel good about yourself, you perform better in all aspects of your life.

Q LT *THEOREM*

WHEN YOU FEEL EXHAUSTED IS WHEN YOU NEED TO EXERCISE THE MOST.

You're not depleting yourself if you exercise when you feel tired. Dr. William Friedewald, associate director of the National Institutes of Health, says that people who exercise regularly feel more energy after working out, even if they were tired before starting.

Tips for Exercising

Choose a type of exercise that you enjoy: walking, racquetball, dancing, an exercise or yoga class at the local YMCA, martial arts, or aerobics. You could hire a personal trainer to come to your home. Choose something you like since there will be times when anticipation will be your only motivation.

Choose exercise that fits your lifestyle. If you come home to three eager children after work and feel pressured and guilty going off to a gym, pick a sport that includes your family. Take a walk together as a family. Swim at a local pool and take the children with you.

Integrate exercise at work. I know people who cut their lunch hours short and go for a run. Some actually have business meetings while taking a brisk walk.

Consider joining an exercise group. As with many other areas of self-improvement, support gives an edge.

Exercise at least three times a week without fail. Research has shown that the minimum exercise needed to achieve good cardiovascular conditioning is twenty minutes three times a week.

Stretching is an extremely important beginning to all exercise. Any sport, aerobics, running, and even weightlifting must begin with stretching your muscles to avoid injury. Yoga, too, is a great exercise for breathing, flexibility, and body alignment.

Build strength. Work muscles for definition and increasing muscle mass. Free weights, dumbbells, and barbells are one choice, rowing machines another. There are machines on the market that serve the same purpose as free weights.

Exercise for cardiovascular conditioning. The obvious choice is jogging or fast walking, but there is cross-country skiing, stair-climbing, chopping wood, dancing, racquetball, rowing, tennis, biking, and swimming. Before you choose, be sure to consult your physician.

Vary your exercise program. It keeps you from getting bored. Also, after a long period of the same exercise routine, your body adapts and improvement slows down. So shake things up. Swim if you are used to lifting weights, or play racquetball instead of running.

Q L T *THEOREM*

YOU ARE WHAT YOU EAT.

The wrong foods deplete your body of energy. When you create a solid image of your ideal body, your intuition will let you know what foods you need, but this takes time.

You need fresh fruits, fresh vegetables, nuts, and whole grains. I am not a strict vegetarian, but I eliminated all red meat from my diet years ago. I love pasta with vegetables. I eat fish and skinless white meat of turkey or chicken.

There are plenty of books on nutrition. Pick one up and use it to develop your own nutritional plan. Better yet, consult a doctor or a nutritionist, too.

QUANTUM LEAP STRATEGIES FOR FINANCIAL SECURITY

> If you focus your attention on the lack of money, that's what will get reinforced. Where you put your mental attention is what gets nourished. Poverty comes to the person who is emotionally and intellectually prepared for it. Prosperity is attracted to the person who is emotionally and intellectually ready to accept it, expect it, and enjoy it.
>
> —JERRY GILLES,
> as quoted by David Gershon and Gail Straub,
> *Empowerment: The Art of Creating*
> *Your Life as You Want It*

Your beliefs about scarcity and abundance directly influence the financial choices you make: You may decide not to take a job because the pay is lower or the hours are longer; you may be accustomed to being taken care of; or you might sincerely believe you're not good enough for the kind of job you dream of. Can you change your mind-set? I believe you can.

> Wealth is the product of a man's capacity to think.
> —AYN RAND,
> American writer

1. Do you live your life from scarcity or abundance?

Scarcity is fear-based. It's thinking there is not enough to go around. Scarcity can stem from believing money is wrong, or that you're not good enough to have it. Scarcity is denying one-third of the very foundation upon which Quantum Leap Thinking is built: your creative potential.

Belief in abundance is a leap of faith. It is the belief that you can always create what money you need and you possess all the resources you need. That belief will give you energy.

2. Do you believe money is good or bad, spiritual or unspiritual?

Some of us look at money as if it were some living, breathing entity capable of good and bad acts, but money is what we *project* on it. True wealth is a state of mind.

3. How much is enough?

Get past what other people think and decide for yourself. You may choose to live a simple life that demands little in the way of money. How much is enough for you and the life you've chosen? Create the amount of money you need to support the life you want.

Affirmations can be a powerful help. I suspect they are a mild form of self-hypnosis and make us aware of opportunities to which we might otherwise be blind. Affirmations, like the ones below, are positive statements of possibility. Choose one and repeat it during the day, while you're commuting, bathing the baby, dialing the phone. Affirmations are a great adjunct to visualization.

- I am creating financial independence in my life.
- I deserve prosperity.

- Money allows me to manifest my vision.
- Money allows me to manifest my spiritual ideas.
- I allow money to flow to me effortlessly.

My personal favorite is "Great prosperity is flowing in my direction." It's a trigger to reaffirm my positive beliefs about wealth.

However, the greatest secret to financial wealth is the obvious: Create something of value. Look for a need and fill it, but begin with yourself. Consider how you can make yourself more valuable.

> Make all you can, save all you can, give all you can.
> —JOHN WESLEY,
> English theologian, evangelist,
> and founder of Methodism

QUANTUM LEAP STRATEGIES FOR QUALITY RELATIONSHIPS

> Love is the medicine for the sickness of mankind. We can live if we have love.
> —DR. KARL MENNINGER,
> American psychiatrist

Think about the books and poetry you have read, and the movies and television programs you have seen. What force is almost always at work? Almost always, it's the struggle to love.

Relationships venture into the heart. A relationship touches the very center of what it means to be human, but when we choose to open ourselves up, we risk being hurt. Loving makes some people feel out of control.

Look around you. How many unhappy partnerships do you see? How many people do you know who are seeking a nurturing, loving relationship? Why is it so hard?

Many of my friends have discovered *A Course in Miracles*, created and published by the Foundation for Inner Peace, which teaches that all communication is either a loving response or a cry for help. Imagine how your perception of communication and relationships would change if you were to incorporate that simple statement into your belief system.

Seeing the world through the filter of love melts away negativity. If someone confronts you, your gentle response would eventually override your attacker's anger. That would indeed be a miracle. It would also be magic.

Unconditional Love

Do you want to be right, or do you want to be happy?
—DR. GERALD JAMPOLSKY,
Love Is Letting Go of Fear

If you get good grades, you will be loved; bad grades, you won't. It's no wonder that love is confusing. We've been conditioned to love those who are good and do good things, ourselves included. If expectations are not met, love is threatened or withheld. Love becomes conditional.

Unfortunately the map we use to determine how love works is often marked with false information and erroneous assumptions. Nevertheless, it's the only map we have.

Imagine that only two emotions exist: love and fear. Once you get rid of fear, there is only love left.

1. Love Yourself First.

In Edmond Rostand's play *Cyrano de Bergerac*, the title character says, "I long ago made the decision that in every area of life, I will choose the path of least resistance in this, that I will please at least myself in all things." This was Cyrano's reply when asked why he should refuse to compromise his principles for anyone. When you do what feels right for yourself, you have integrity. Put yourself at the top of the list of people for whose happiness, joy, health, and well-being you are responsible. You are the only person who can dictate what makes you happy.

This does not mean being self-centered or narcissistic. When you nurture a healthy relationship with yourself, you create the foundation for other loving relationships. The more you forgive yourself for your shortcomings, the easier it is to forgive others for theirs. There are enough hurdles to challenge a relationship without adding the strain of your own neediness and desperation.

Hans Selye, researcher and author on stress, used the term *altruistic selfishness.* He asserts that before we can take care of anyone else, we must take care of ourselves. It's only a small leap to realize that in order to love others, we must first love ourselves. How can you give what you don't have?

2. Acknowledge Your Fears About Love.

The idea of committing to a relationship or the feeling of being in love can tap into some of your most basic fears. If you associate fear with relationships, go through the following exercise.

a. Go into your most relaxed state.

b. Imagine telling someone you love him or her or imagine being told that you are loved.

c. Feel the fear fully with all your senses. Do you feel more than one fear? If so, see if you can discover the basic fear that supports the other fears.

d. Give the fear a shape, form, color, and texture. Describe it as fully as you can.

e. Accept the possibility that you have created the fear.

f. If you can create fear, you can create fearlessness, too. Create a fearless relationship in your imagination. How would you like it to look and feel? What images and emotions come to mind? What circumstances exist in your visualization? What words would you use to describe your ideal relationship?

g. Surround yourself with your ideal relationship. Live it. Breathe it. See it. Feel it. Open your heart. Visualize it, then visualize it again.

h. Record in your journal, in the greatest of detail, the exact picture of your ideal relationship. As you write, become aware of any resistance.

3. Accept People as They Are.

People sometimes enter a relationship believing that the other person will change, that one partner will be able to influence the other's behavior. That is a surefire formula for failure.

Instead, respect the needs of the individual in your relationship. Take the time to discover the core values of your partner and make sure those values are honored.

Confrontations are an integral part of the dynamics of any meaningful, committed relationship. The healthy solution is for both individuals to express what they want and need and to confront the situation. With any power conflict, clear and precise negotiation is the only solution.

Accept responsibility for the way you feel and ask for what you need. Often your partner hasn't a clue that he or she has hurt your feelings or irritated you. You need to ask for what you want in a way that doesn't cause a defensive response:

"I'm sure you didn't mean to hurt me, but I feel hurt."

"I know you're busy, but I need to spend some time with you."

"When you said that, I was hurt and I know that wasn't your intention."

4. Tell the Truth.

Q LT *THEOREM*

HONEST COMMUNICATION IS THE BASIS OF ALL LOVING, HEALTHY RELATIONSHIPS.

Honesty can be very uncomfortable. It's easier to confide our deepest upsets and hurts to our barber, hairdresser, or mechanic than it is to the ones we love.

Avoid the Accumulation Effect. It is easy to let little irritations and resentments slide. We don't want to hurt people's feelings, we don't want to look foolish, we don't want to make a mountain out of a molehill. However, not communicating what may appear meaningless has what I call the Accumulation Effect. The pressure builds as the little frustrations accumulate until there is an explosion of emotion. Whatever caused the explosion is seldom the real reason.

If one too many raindrops fall on a leaf, the leaf gives way, unable to support the weight of the rain. In a relationship, the drops of small hurts accumulate, and the slightest irritation can trigger the Accumulation Effect. Arguments happen that have nothing to do with what has just occurred but have everything to do with what has been stored up from the past. Angry words are exchanged that may permanently damage the relationship.

All this could have been avoided had there been healthy communication.

Q LT *THEOREM*

MAJOR PROBLEMS IN RELATIONSHIPS CAN BE AVOIDED BY INSTANTLY COMMUNICATING WHAT MAY APPEAR TO BE SMALL PROBLEMS.

5. Share the Bad as Well as the Good.

Upon returning from a speaking engagement late one night, I received a horrible shock. The daughter of one of my closest friends had left a message on my answering machine that her mother had passed away that afternoon.

Although she lived three thousand miles away, she had been part of my life for thirty years. She was both friend and mentor. Throughout the night, I kept waking up with feelings of profound loss and deep sadness.

I called the daughter the next day. My friend had been very ill for some time and she didn't want to let me know because it would have worried me. I hung up the phone, hurt and disappointed. I hadn't had the chance to say good-bye. Not only did I feel left out, but I didn't have the opportunity to support my dear friend during her illness. I wasn't able to be at her bedside when she died, which may have given her comfort.

When it comes to close partnerships, the bad must be shared with the good. The good and the bad make up the whole.

6. Renew Relationships on a Consistent Basis.

When a relationship is in its formative stage, both parties spend a great deal of time talking. They give unexpected gifts, bring flowers, and send cards. They treat potential partners with respect, listening to problems, sharing, being empathetic. Then something peculiar begins to take place.

As the relationship matures, we begin to expect certain behavior. We criticize more, show appreciation less, get angry more easily, have less patience, and spend less time listening. We forget what brought us together in the first place. The arrogance of assumption sets in: We believe our partner will be there forever, regardless of what we do or say.

Relationships take work. Make it a daily practice to think of all the shared values that brought you together in the first place. Treat your partner as a friend. Respect and value that friendship on a consistent basis. Take the time to listen. Take the time to do the thoughtful little things that made a difference at the beginning of your relationship.

Take the time in the morning or before you go to bed to renew that respect. Give that extra hug. Have the extra patience. Take a few moments to ask how your partner is doing/feeling, and then listen.

Look at a partnership as a team. The sum is greater than the parts. When two people form a commitment, a metaphorical third person is formed. The energy and chemistry of the two form a synergistic third party that needs as much nurturing as does each of the parts separately.

7. Have Fun.

Playfulness is an important part of any relationship. Just as you must schedule time to be alone, you must also schedule time to play. Enjoy each other. After all, why did you choose the relationship in the first place?

▨ QUANTUM LEAP STRATEGIES FOR CAREER

> Work should be more fun than fun.
>
> —SIR NOEL COWARD,
> English actor and playwright

I had dinner with the president of a large corporation and a group of his senior managers. We talked about a number of things, including the importance of the work environment and methods of employee motivation, and then our conversation drifted into more personal topics. It was stimulating primarily because the president was excited about his work and his life. He was both interesting and interested.

He shared many of the fears that he had to overcome and the risks he had taken on his way to the presidency. He said he had recently healed his relationship with his son. We talked about travel, books, and dreams. I was impressed with his candor.

Suddenly the conversation came to a halt. I assumed we had exhausted our subject matter, but I saw a look of melancholy pass over his face. "You know what makes me sad?" he said. "I look around me and the majority of people I meet have tombstones in their eyes. Don't they realize how short life is? Why don't they do what makes them happy?"

> Do your job naturally because you like it and success will take care of itself.
> —DR. NORMAN VINCENT PEALE,
> American theologian and philosopher

When our work and our values are mismatched, we pay a huge price. We can all justify the jobs we have chosen, but the quality of our lives can be thrown out of balance when too much focus and energy is put on our jobs, even if the work is fun.

> If it doesn't absorb you, if it isn't any fun, don't do it.
> —D. H. LAWRENCE,
> English novelist

Sometimes you get so locked up in your work that you see it as separate from the rest of your life but necessary for survival. You may feel you have no control over what you're doing and how to do it. Or maybe you have simply lost sight of your dreams.

You have far more control over your work than you realize. You have the power to change how you view your work. You have the power to build meaning into it. You have the power to find or create a job that makes you feel complete.

Perhaps you could move to a different position within your company, or maybe you can reengineer your job so that it's more fun and gives you a feeling of making a difference. Or you can create the ideal job, one that matches your greatest dream.

Before any of this is possible, however, you have to know what you want. Why did you choose the job in the first place? Why do you work at all?

> The test of a vocation is the love of the drudgery it involves.
>
> —LOGAN P. SMITH,
> English novelist

Get specific and actually think about what the word *work* means to you, what you want from your work, and what you get in return. Do you feel you make a contribution?

Put your current job on your own personal balance scale. What does your job provide you with? What does it lack?

Review your values. What can you do to make your present job more in balance with your values?

Q LT *THEOREM*

PEOPLE PERFORM AT THEIR BEST WHEN CONTRIBUTING THEIR TALENTS TO SOMETHING THEY BELIEVE IN.

Research has shown that there are three primary reasons people work: money, affiliation, and purpose. Money is an obvious motivator. Affiliation is obvious, too. People need to feel connected to others. It provides them with a sense of belonging and an opportunity for recognition.

But the third reason people work is the key to productivity. People who excel have a sense of purpose. They feel their work makes a difference. They feel they have made a contribution to something greater than themselves.

Let go of everything you previously thought impossible or impractical. Forget your experience or training and ignore the image you have of yourself. Challenge your assumptions and stretch your imagination. You can do anything you desire, but you need to choose something.

If you enjoy reading, perhaps you could have a job reading manuscripts for publishers or scripts for movies. If you enjoy working with your hands, perhaps you can make furniture. The definition of your ideal job is limited only by your imagination.

TAKING INVENTORY

An acorn dreamed of being a beautiful pine tree when he grew up. The acorn was given a book on positive thinking and he diligently read it, following all the advice on using positive thinking to achieve your dreams. But as the acorn grew, he felt himself changing into something very different from a pine tree.

The acorn accumulated every book on visualization and change that he could find. He followed the exercises faithfully. The acorn spent hours visualizing himself as a pine tree. But despite all his efforts, that acorn grew into a massive, elegant oak tree.

The metaphor is simple. You are who you are. You have certain God-given traits that are unique to you. There is no one else walking the face of this Earth with your mental, emotional, spiritual, and physical makeup.

To jump-start your self-inventory process, take a realistic, honest look at yourself and list your strengths and weaknesses on paper. Look them over and cross out what you consider the negative aspects of your makeup. Then play to your strengths.

To reach your fullest potential, you must not waste precious time trying to be what you are not. If you're an oak, you don't want to waste a lifetime trying to be a pine tree. You want to become the greatest and most magnificent oak tree you can.

> Do not think your truth can be found by anyone else; be ashamed of nothing more than of that.
> —ANDRÉ GIDE,
> French novelist

Q L T *THEOREM*

QUANTUM LEAP THINKERS ACCEPT THEIR WEAKNESSES AND FOCUS ON THEIR STRENGTHS.

CELEBRATE YOURSELF

Set your modesty aside. Take that list of all your good points and put them where you can see them. Write them in your journal, tape them on the front of the refrigerator, or write them on the wall of the garage with a crayon. Acknowledge the goodness, wisdom, and specialness of yourself. Celebrate who you are. Appreciate yourself.

> Do what you know, and perception is converted into character.
> —RALPH WALDO EMERSON

THE "I AM . . ." EXERCISE

Write "I am . . ." at the top of a page in your journal or a notebook and complete the sentence as many times as you can with whatever comes to your mind. Write for ten minutes. Keep your pencil moving. Cover every aspect of your life from your superficial feelings to your deepest emotions, from your self-image to your love of nature. Include talents, characteristics, and personality traits. If you get stuck, invent some.

EXERCISES IN MORTALITY

Perhaps the best cure for the fear of death is to reflect that life has a beginning as well as an end. There was a time when we

were not; this gives us no concern. Why then trouble us that a
time will come when we shall cease to be?
—WILLIAM HAZLITT,
English essayist

1. Draw a spiral. Imagine the beginning of the spiral is birth.
   At the end of the spiral, write the number of years you think
   you will live and place a dot at the point in the spiral that
   represents your present age. Draw a horizontal line through
   the dot.
      Look at the length of time you have left in this life. How
   do you want the rest of your life to look?
2. Write your own epitaph, one sentence that represents the
   essence of who you are and what people will read about you
   forever.
      It's not fair to write, "I told you I was sick." Make it heart-
   felt. How would you like to be remembered?
3. Write your own eulogy. Include what you think people will
   say about you, your outstanding characteristics, and your
   contributions to your family and to the community. Write
   the eulogy exactly as you would like to hear it delivered.
4. What contributions have you made in your lifetime? What
   have you always dreamed of contributing? Looking at the
   spiral of your life, ask yourself what you want to contribute
   in the time remaining, and write it down.
5. What do you want most from life? Keep your response short
   and simple.

There is nothing like dreams to create the future, Utopia today,
flesh and blood tomorrow.
—VICTOR HUGO

Over the years I have had some fantastic dreams, things I
wanted to do and be in the future. They weren't goals; they were
dreams.

I dreamed of owning a second home in the Virgin Islands. The
dream certainly wasn't practical: I had no money, and my family
had no money to lend me. But I wouldn't let it go.

I managed to save enough money to make a small down payment on a condominium. It took me five years, but I made my dream come true.

Since then I've created three separate careers, worked on a world cruise, earned my hot-air ballooning license, and acted in films and on television. I've traveled all over the world speaking to audiences, and I've raced cars on a professional racetrack. These were all dreams, but none of them would have come true had I not dreamed them in the first place.

Q L T *THEOREM*

THE FREEDOM TO DREAM AND REACH FOR DREAMS IS THE ESSENCE OF QUANTUM LEAP THINKING.

There is nothing to stop you from making your dreams come true. Set aside all sense of being practical. Don't concern yourself with how you're going to do it. Making dreams come true has no rules.

EXERCISE IN DREAMING

If your life could be any way you wanted it, how would you choose it to be? If you could do, be, or own anything you wanted, what would you do, what would you be, what would you have?

Consider the following categories as you think about that:

- Personal Improvement
- Family and Relationships
- Career
- Adventure
- Spiritual
- Contribution and Charity

Take at least ten minutes and list all the dreams you can imagine. Do your best to come up with a minimum of seventy, and when you are done, you will have done what most of us never dare to do: acknowledged your dreams. This is the first step to making them come true.

CREATING YOUR OWN GRAND VISION

Now that you have completed your dream list, you can start laying the foundation for your Grand Vision. Recall the elements of a Grand Vision.

A Grand Vision is:

1. always about others.
2. idealistic and spiritual.
3. authentic and genuine.
4. extraordinary.
5. from the heart and creates passion.
6. based on your values.

Recall your six core values. The six elements of a Grand Vision, your six core values, and the list of dreams you just made are all you need to create your own personal vision.

I'll share mine with you. I hope it will give you support in forming yours.

> I am dedicated to helping others improve the quality of their lives and the lives of everyone with whom they come in contact. I do my utmost to open up new possibilities. I am committed to provide opportunities, encouragement, hope, and self-motivation to others. I intend to communicate through love with integrity, honesty, and openness. Above all else, I am loyal to my family and close friends. I am committed to bringing a sense of playfulness, joy, and fun to life. My job is to make the world a better place.
>
> —JAMES J. MAPES,
> January 1995

Take your time creating your Grand Vision. It may take you a week, a month, or more. I still change or add to mine. Keep it flexible.

Your Grand Vision locks in place the rubber band around your compelling future. This cre-

> Laughter, play, and fun cross-flow within all our basic needs and are a necessary part of balance in your life.

ates drive for your goals and provides you with the tension to move you in right direction. Don't mistake tension for stress. Quantum Tension creates energy, excitement, and drive.

FROM ME TO WE

TEAMS: THE QUANTUM LEAP PARTNERSHIP

None of us is as smart as all of us.

—Anonymous

A merican culture has glorified rugged individualism. We praise individual achievement and singular excellence. Parents, teachers, and coaches emphasize individual accomplishment, which in turn shows up in organizational thinking. We look out for number one.

Think about our educational system. Students are discouraged from sharing information. That's cheating. We are urged to find out what we do best and then compete against our peers. We focus on the winner, even when he or she could not have succeeded without the help of his or her class, group, or team.

On one hand, we are taught that competition brings out the best in people; and on the other hand, we are told that we should cooperate and work together as a team. Are individualism and teamwork at cross purposes? Could it be that competition ultimately does more damage than cooperation?

We form partnerships for many different reasons. We form loving relationships, friendships, and marriages. We collaborate to compose music or write screenplays. The concept presents limitless possibilities. The recent partnering of two mammoth computer companies and two entertainment giants suggests a new, exciting strategy for the business world. Partnerships are nothing more than the genesis of the concept of teams.

A team is a small group of people with compatible and complementary skills committed to a common vision and specific, identifiable goals. Members of self-directed teams typically plan and schedule work, make production-related decisions, handle job assignments, and take the actions necessary to solve problems. The team members must be committed to working together to achieve the team's vision and support the vision of the organization.

Q LT *THEOREM*

TEAMS ARE OUR GREATEST TOOL TO PRODUCE QUANTUM LEAPS WITH SPEED.

While teams may help create a quantum leap, the mechanics of developing successful teams requires time, patience, energy, commitment, knowledge, superb communication skills, and tremendous resources. Perhaps because of this, the actual implementation of teams is not as widespread as you might think.

According to *Fortune* magazine (September 5, 1994), the Center for Effective Organizations at the University of Southern California recently conducted a survey of Fortune 1000 companies showing that 68 percent use self-managed or high-performance teams, but only 10 percent of workers are in such teams. USC's Edward Lawler, the management professor who oversaw the study, says, "Teams are the Ferraris of work design. They're high-performance, but high-maintenance and expensive."

Q LT *THEOREM*

TRUE TEAMING REQUIRES TOTAL COMMITMENT AND A FUNDAMENTAL CHANGE OF MIND-SET FOR MANAGEMENT.

Teamwork is often met with overwhelming resistance. Many of us don't like to work on teams. Some are loners who contribute best when left to work on their own. Others feel that teams are time-consuming, expensive, uncertain, or risky.

The arguments against forming teams are similar, regardless of who's complaining. Workers say that management will not give them the power to make decisions. Students say teachers don't give them freedom. People are uncomfortable participating in a group, or they don't want to depend on others. They feel embarrassed or conspicuous. Or they might say they don't have the time, or it's too complicated, or they don't want to work with a bunch of strangers. Given this negativity, teams are doomed. Teamwork does not come naturally.

Basic human fears enter the picture: the fear of speaking up in a group, the fear of being punished for the mistakes of others, and the fear of having to be forced to agree with opposite points of view. People often resist being part of a team when they are not the leaders.

We do have team models. Our parents and teachers have instructed us in teamwork values. Most sports are team sports. We read books like *The Three Musketeers* and see movies like the *Star Trek* series and television shows like "Star Trek: The Next Generation," "Voyager," and "Deep Space Nine," where teams vanquish seemingly impossible odds. Theatrical productions also depend on successful teamwork.

I participated in a program for a large paper products company. The two-day conference was based on the movie *The Magnificent Seven*. The plan was to create a supercharged selling team in a specialty market. The team members, like the seven men in the movie, were presented with a phenomenal challenge on which their very survival was based.

Nevertheless, the concept of teamwork takes a backseat to individual responsibility and self-preservation. We're reluctant to trust others, and the illusion of separability remains the dominant paradigm.

The most destructive model we have for teams is sports. Sports are fun, healthy, and great entertainment, but they promote competition, not cooperation. However, within athletics can be found the elements vital to self-directed and high-performance teams:

namely, striving for personal excellence, coaching, and commitment.

Perhaps volleyball comes closest to the best sports model for teams. Each player must assume the place of every other member of the team at some time during the game, so everyone has to be proficient in each position. The team captain serves as a source of strength rather than control. It's close to an ideal team, but for our purposes, not quite.

Remember what happens when a hologram is divided into a number of pieces? Each piece contains the information of the whole from a slightly different perspective. I call the model team a *Holographic Team*.

I have a wonderful example of a Holographic Team at work. My friend Donald Granger, a senior executive vice president at Paramount Studios, gave me a box of *Star Trek* souvenirs for Christmas one year. I love anything to do with *Star Trek*, and I thanked him warmly, but he asked me if I was ready for the rest of my gift. He asked if I would like to be in the next *Star Trek* movie, *Star Trek VI*.

I couldn't believe it. He was offering me a dream.

"Would you like to be a Klingon?"

Absolutely!

Weeks later I stood expectantly in the fitting room. I looked over to my right and spied Christopher Plummer in Klingon makeup. I felt very special, like a real movie star.

This vision of myself was shattered a few minutes later when the wardrobe lady asked me if I would be willing to shave off my eyebrows.

I was going to do a presentation for IBM in two weeks. I really couldn't see myself giving a serious program on managing change and thinking outside the box without my eyebrows. I was devastated. I didn't want to shave them, and I told her so.

She stared at me in astonishment. "What kind of an actor are you?"

"I guess I'm an actor who won't shave off his eyebrows."

"Oh dear, oh dear," she mumbled. She disappeared behind a rack of costumes. I wondered if I was going to be fired before I even got fitted, but within moments she returned with a large cape and a very strange-looking hat. "Would you like to be a Zelonite?"

What was a Zelonite?

She dressed me and nudged me in front of a mirror. "Of course, you'll have a blue face."

"Of course," I replied. I knew nothing about a blue face, and the costume was anything but flattering. I looked like a bag lady, and I guessed I was going to be a bag lady with a blue face.

I was instructed to arrive for my makeup at three o'clock in the morning. I am not a morning person. Waiting in line with the other actors, I questioned my sanity, but my doubts were dispelled when the crew of the Starship *Enterprise* appeared. This was my dream come true.

For the next week I watched the production staff, makeup team, lighting crew, assistant directors, and director Nicholas Meyer at work. I watched as problem after problem was surmounted. Nicholas was the ultimate cheerleader, pulling hidden resources out of an exhausted cast and crew. I asked him once how he was able to find the energy to cope with everything, from the breakdown of a generator, which drove production costs up by the second, to script problems and ego clashes. "I love people," he told me.

Through the haze of my exhaustion on my flight back to New York, I realized that I had just been part of a true Holographic Team. Moviemaking is a great model for high-performance, self-managed teams in action. There was a central vision to which hundreds of individuals were aligned. Information flowed from one department to another. Everyone was highly trained. People solved problems in any department, always keeping the final outcome in mind.

Everyone was committed to a strong vision (a successful production), and there were several self-managed teams that supported the whole (i.e., costumes, set design, lighting, script, director). There were potentially damaging egos and conflict, but the vision was almost always strong enough to surmount whatever challenges arose.

The going wasn't easy. Conflict popped up all over the place, but it was handled with clear, consistent communication.

CHECK ONE:
Teams work:

    a. _____ always.
    b. _____ never.
    c. _____ sometimes.

If you checked C, you were right. Sometimes teams work. Teams are not a magic bullet, but they can create quantum leaps in productivity if we can form them carefully and watch out for the barriers that get in the way.

■ THE BARRIERS TO SUCCESSFUL TEAMWORK

Lack of Vision.

A team must have a compelling purpose that appeals both emotionally and rationally to the members of the team. If the team lacks a vision, its members lack vision.

Lack of Commitment.

Many people think teams don't make a difference except in times of trouble and unpredictable circumstance. Others think teams take up too much time, require too much maintenance, or slow up decision making. Still others believe in teams as a concept, but fail to follow up, thinking that teams function without support.

Teams fulfill their functions only in an environment of total commitment.

Confusing Teams With Teamwork.

The words *team* and *teamwork* are often used interchangeably, but groups working together do not magically become a team. Some organizations think an annual convention will motivate the entire group to work together as a team, but an organization can never be a team. They can, however, practice teamwork.

Teams and teamwork are vastly different.

Teamwork is a set of values adopted by a group. Teamwork

encourages respect for the dignity of the individual, embraces diversity, and supports superior communication. Teamwork provides support, resources, and recognition. While these teamwork values are necessary to high-performance teams, they do not by themselves create a team.

Lack of Training.

Self-directed, high-performance, and cross-functional teams require greater skills. People often get caught up in team-mania. They throw together a group of people and expect them to produce results. But teams require global thinking, systems thinking, change management, decision making, conflict resolution, problem solving, communication, and technology. Somebody has to provide training.

Control, Manipulation, and Fear.

A team must have freedom. The very nature of a high-performance team demands that it be trusted and empowered.

Competition.

The assumption that competition increases performance is erroneous and short-sighted. Competition among team members, managers and teams, supervisors and teams, or teams within the same organization is destructive.

The Wrong Kind of Team.

It all started with the Quality Circles of the 1980s. Composed of workers and supervisors, Quality Circles met periodically to discuss workplace problems. Unfortunately, Quality Circles exist primarily where leadership is afraid to let go of control. Although still in existence, Quality Circles are on the decline, but they served the purpose of bringing to light the potential value of self-directed teams. While Quality Circles may have supported small gains in productivity, they will never provide quantum leaps.

Today there are Virtual Teams, where members talk by

computer and take turns playing the role of leader. There are Management Teams made up of managers from various departments, which basically coordinate work among other teams; Work Teams, which handle day-to-day problems; and Problem-solving Teams, which come together until a specific problem is solved and then disband. There are Cross-functional Teams, which are made up of several departments like manufacturing, research and development, engineering, and finance.

Work Teams are the button-pushers. Work Teams are also known as high-performance, self-managed, or self-directed teams. In addition to doing the day-to-day work, a Work Team is empowered with the authority to make decisions on how the daily work is done. If a work team is genuinely empowered, it has a budget and the authority to determine the order in which designated tasks are done. While some members may come and go, Work Teams tend to be permanent, and it is the Work Team that ignites the energy to take quantum leaps in a team environment.

So before you rush off to form Work Teams, ask yourself, "Do I really need a team?"

Analyze the task at hand. Can it be done faster by a person working alone? Does the work really require people to interact with each other? It's a mistake to get people to work together simply for the sake of working together.

Ed O'Brien, director of education and training at Corning, Inc., explains the reasoning process behind the commitment to go through the stress, effort, and expense of developing and supporting a team approach. "Evolutionary changes were no longer adequate. It was not sufficient to keep tweaking our process to improve production yields by two percent a year. The environment demanded revolutionary changes." Revolutionary changes need the power found only in the collective consciousness of a team.

QLT *THEOREM*

TEAMS MUST EVOLVE THROUGH A NATURAL ORGANIC PROCESS.

Professor Paul Osterman of MIT's Sloan School says, "When teams are introduced in combination with other organization changes, they work. When they're introduced as an isolated practice, they fail. . . . Most are introduced in isolation." Teams must be considered an integral part of one system.

At the genesis of the team process, the following questions must be carefully considered: Does the organization support the processes and values of the team? Does the team support the processes and values of the organization? For success, the answer must be "yes" to both questions.

The mind-set of the Holographic Team is a major paradigm shift from "me" to "we" and includes all the support points of empowerment that go with it. When the "we" paradigm is in place, challenges will work themselves out. Synergy, the acid test of teamwork, will propel the whole to unexpected heights.

The role of the team leader is neither to control nor to allow team members to slough off their responsibilities. The team will directly reflect the quality of its leadership. Therefore, the team leader must be a master at diplomacy, persuasion, communication, and conflict resolution. Let's imagine that all elements for a Holographic Team are in place.

A successful Holographic Team exhibits:

Consistency.

A Holographic Team cannot develop where team members interact sporadically or occasionally. Just like a physical workout program, results demand consistency.

Acknowledgment.

In order to create commitment, team members must know they make a difference. The group must be empowered to make things happen and see the results. If team members don't feel pride in their work, you will soon have a dysfunctional team or no team at all.

Patience.

Take it slowly. Start with a single team as a pilot project. Get the feel of relinquishing control. Learn about empowerment. Begin with a relatively simple issue and see how the team performs. Get to know your players, and give the people on the sidelines a break.

Flexibility.

A leader must have a strong, compelling vision. However, that vision must be flexible enough for team members to create owner-ship through developing their own vision. If you have made a uni-lateral decision that you insist on keeping, don't waste your time forming a team.

Cooperation.

I suggest you read *No Contest: The Case Against Competition* by Alfie Kohn. Kohn says, "Competing for a job or a plate of food is a reasonable choice only if we restrict our vision to the situation as it exists in a given instant—if we disregard causes, conse-quences, and context."

Job Rotation.

Job rotation balances the workload, stretches the learning curve, and breaks down tensions and barriers among members. The more often jobs are rotated, the better the team's morale and the greater the productivity. Although there may be resistance to changing responsibilities, the pressure imposed on team members to learn new skills increases self-confidence and enhances the un-derstanding of the system, process, and business. In effect, job rotation nurtures the creative spirit.

Reward.

Reward systems are one of the sticking points of team develop-ment. There is no set model for team compensation. The challenge stems from emphasizing team productivity over individual per-formance, yet job rotation requires team members to learn new skills, and those individuals expect to be compensated.

We must make a shift in recognition programs from the senior-ity of the individual to the productivity of the team. That is not to say that outstanding individuals shouldn't be recognized, but rather that the mind-set of recognition and compensation must shift to the individual who contributes most effectively to the team who contributes most.

The challenge of creating successful Holographic Teams becomes obvious in my workshops. Even though I spend two hours setting up a "no competition" atmosphere, teams invariably end up competing in the team-building exercises. They could create something magnificent if they would combine forces and cooperate, but they remain separate and competitive. They limit their potential.

This, then, is another challenge for the visionary leader: to turn competition into cooperation.

THE CHALLENGE OF
LEADERSHIP

The only way leaders can make values tangible and real to followers is through their behaviors and actions. Employees look to their leaders as role models of how they should behave. And when in doubt, they believe actions over words, without fail.

—JOHN W. GARDNER,
On Leadership

hink about a high school dance. There are the students who rush to the dance floor. When the band starts playing, they're immediately dancing. Standing around the perimeter of the dance floor is another group. They want to be out there, but they are waiting to be invited.

There's a third group slouching against the walls. They're interested, and maybe they can be coaxed out on the floor. The fourth group stays in the parking lot, sitting in their cars or on their motorcycles. They make fun of the students inside.

Leaders face the same scenario. Some people will instantly jump on the bandwagon, and some will never buy into the idea. Leaders must be aware of where to focus their energies. The group poised on the edge of commitment and the group slouching against the wall require the greatest amount of focus, but these two groups can be brought into the fold with some enthusiastic support from the group already on the dance floor.

Q LT *THEOREM*

A LEADER MUST MODEL THE VISION CONSISTENTLY IN A HIGHLY VIABLE, CONSISTENT, AND ETHICAL MANNER.

> As for the best leaders, the people do not notice their existence. The next best, the people honor and praise. The next, the people fear; and the next, the people hate. When the best leaders' work is done, the people say, "We did it ourselves."
> —LAO-TZU

Ralph Stayer, CEO of Johnsonville Foods, said, "The very things that brought me success—my centralized control, my aggressive behavior, my authoritarian business practices—were creating the environment that made me so unhappy. If I wanted to improve results, I had to increase their [the employees'] involvement in the business."

A visionary leader invents new rules and generates selling, manufacturing, marketing, parenting, teaching, and training by creating an entirely new way of thinking, devoid of control, because creative thinking, risk taking, innovation, and productivity thrive only in an environment of freedom and safety.

Like it or not, we are part of a global community. A Holographic Global Partnership is forming and will continue to shape and reinvent itself. Our environment takes a daily pounding, and we are just beginning to acquire enough information about the damage that has been done. Our educational system must acknowledge and embrace new methodologies of teaching interactive learning, computer technology, and global electronic communication. Health care systems are under attack and must reinvent themselves to survive. The signals for a new way of thinking are obvious even to those who want to close their eyes and pretend that everything will be as it once was.

Countries once considered vastly separate are realizing they are an integral part of the world. They are slowly becoming aware that their very survival depends on the survival of others. Never before on all fronts has the world been more desperately in need of inspired leadership—leadership that is based on making a difference, Quantum Leap Values, and Grand Vision.

How many of you would have followed me across that bed of hot coals had I started screaming or if I had leaped off at the halfway point? Not many, I assure you.

I walked because the person in front of me walked, and the woman behind me walked because I walked, and the man behind her walked because she walked. Each one of us unconsciously took the role of leadership for the person following.

People watch and model your behavior. You influence others as you are influenced. That's the way humans act. You may resist your personal power, but the truth is apparent in relationships of all kinds. If you are a parent, observe your children. If you are a manager or supervisor, watch the behavior of your employees. If you are a CEO, step back and notice the attitudes of management. You may be surprised to find yourself looking in the mirror of your creation.

Like it or not, by our mere presence, we influence others in a positive or negative direction. And like it or not, in that sense we are all leaders. On the micro level, we do in fact have a place as leaders. On the macro level, there are certain traits that define a Quantum Leap leader.

Warren Bennis—psychologist, sociologist, economist, USC professor, former university president, and author of numerous books on the subject of leadership—has spent years studying leaders, the majority of whom are corporate heads.

In the September 1994 issue of *Fortune* magazine, he presents seven characteristics that he believes define a leader:

1. **Business literacy:**
   Does he (or she) know the business? Does he (or she) know the real feel of it?
2. **People skills:**
   Does he (or she) have the capacity to motivate, to bring out the best in people?
3. **Conceptual skills:**
   Does he (or she) have the capacity to think systematically, creatively, and inventively?

4. **Track record:**
   Has he (or she) done it before and done it well?
5. **Taste:**
   Does he (or she) have the ability to pick the right people—not clones of himself (or herself) but people who can make up for his (or her) deficiencies?
6. **Judgment:**
   Does he (or she) have the ability to make quick decisions with imperfect data?
7. **Character:**
   The core competency of leadership is character, but character and judgment are the qualities that we know least about when trying to teach them to others.

Bennis avers that the one indispensable quality of leadership is a clear idea of what he or she wants to do. He states, "All the leaders I know have a strongly defined sense of purpose. And when you have an organization where the people are aligned behind a clearly defined vision or purpose, you get a powerful organization."

Vision, then, is at the heart of all great leadership. The personal vision helps create and becomes part of the organizational, team, or family vision. The personal vision ties into the community vision, the team vision joins in harmony with the organizational vision, and the leader's job is to help the process along, no matter how small or large the circle of influence may be. By embracing and envisioning yourself as a leader, your ability to make a difference expands, the healing process speeds up, and your presence supports positive change for Quantum Leaps.

▨ TWELVE TRAITS OF A QUANTUM LEAP LEADER

1. A Leader Must Be Committed to a Vision.

Commitment must be absolute before you can expect results. If you are not totally and absolutely committed to a vision, the vision cannot be shared.

2. A Leader Must Demonstrate the Vision in Action.

You set the tone. By personally demonstrating the vision with specific, visible actions, you set the stage for empowerment. Analyze specific actions that can be taken to demonstrate the vision. Make a list. Read and reread the core values of the vision and decide how they can be translated into action. Actions do not have to be monumental to be effective, but they must be visible and ongoing. Behavior creates and solidifies attitude. Ask yourself how you would act if the vision had already come into being. That's the way you make it come into being.

3. A Leader Must Have Integrity.

Gandhi advised: "A person cannot do right in one department of life while attempting to do wrong in another. Life is one indivisible whole." Leaders must operate every moment of every day congruent with the core values of his or her personal vision. Take responsibility and be accountable.

4. A Leader Must Lay the Groundwork for a Vision to Take Hold.

Nothing is more detrimental than asking people to change their behavior and their thinking without having the resources available to support them. When the necessary resources are in place, it is like a booming voice from a loudspeaker that shouts, "You see, I do mean business, and I'm here to give you all the support you need!"

5. A Leader Must Be a Master Communicator.

The greatest downfall is assuming that just because you have said it—or written it—the message is understood.

> Communication must include both the transference and understanding of meaning.
>
> —D. D. UMSOT,
> *Understanding Organizational Behavior*

Neil Snyder, James J. Dowd, Jr., and Dianne Morse Houghton write in *Vision, Values and Courage*:

> Successfully communicating even a simple message requires a linked chain of events: the communicator must identify the message she or he wishes to communicate, decide how to express the message (translating the idea into words or symbols), and decide what channel to use to send the message (written, oral, face-to-face, telephone); and the receiver must hear the message and then translate it for understanding, attaching personal meaning to the message. Each step within the process, however, provides an opportunity for the intended message to become distorted.

A Quantum Leap Leader is a great listener. Like a miner panning for gold, a good leader sifts through the mounds of input, decides what information is relevant, and, perhaps most importantly, acts on it. Another message is sent over the loudspeaker: "I'm listening. I care. I'm acting."

The next layer of the communication process is for the leader to provide feedback. A leader must let others know when they are on the right track, when they are doing a good job, and when their actions are supporting the vision. Positive feedback is vital to communication.

Corporate speaker Tom Connellan writes in his book *Interpersonal Feedback, Quality Process*, "Not giving feedback communicates a powerful message. Curiously enough, the message it communicates can have a more negative effect than punishment. It communicates not caring, not noticing, unimportance." This explains why children act up, inviting discipline. Discipline is an indication that their parents care.

We need constant attention and reinforcement, and we will look for subtle meaning in everything. As a Quantum Leap Leader, you want to eliminate assumptions and gossip. The only way to accomplish this is to be accountable for your process of communication.

Studies show that seven out of ten employees in the organization don't speak up if they think their point of view differs from their boss's point of view, even if they firmly believe their boss is wrong; so a leader must create an environment that supports the courage to say no.

Think of creative ways to send out your message. People become accustomed to things quickly. Change gets attention.

6. A Leader Must Be Evangelistic.

Enthusiasm breeds enthusiasm. Enthusiasm creates magic. People get caught up in the spirit if the spirit is there. Be an evangelist. Inspire them.

7. A Leader Must Create an Environment to Grow, Support, and Nurture Intellectual Capital.

Warren Bennis writes,

> [Create] an organizational environment that will be not only fast, focused, flexible, and friendly but also fun. By intellectual capital, I mean know-how, expertise, brainpower, innovation, ideas. All the good CEOs tell me that their major challenge is, "How do I release the brainpower of the people in my company?"
>
> Leaders ask the what and why question, not the how question. Leaders think about empowerment, not control. And the best definition of empowerment is that you don't steal responsibility from people. What employees want most from their leaders . . . is direction and meaning, trust and hope.
>
> Every good leader I have spoken with had willful determination to achieve a set of goals, a set of convictions about what he or she wanted his or her organization to achieve. Everyone had a purpose.

8. A Leader Must Have the Courage to Ask for Support.

Remember those kids at the high school dance standing at the edge of the dance floor? They're waiting to be enticed. They're waiting for support. And sometimes you will need support, too. Ask for it.

9. A Leader Must Share Information.

Proprietary information is no longer viable. People want and need to know what is taking place all the time, so they can see how they fit in the larger picture. Commitment to a shared vision requires that each employee have a feeling of ownership.

10. A Leader Must Engender Trust.

If trust comes easily for you, you have an advantage. If not, you must do the work necessary to learn it. Constancy is imperative. People trust when they know what to expect.

Trust is a two-way street. If a leader has the courage to trust and empower others, then the leader has the right to expect them to be trustworthy. For the most part, placing trust in a person will create trustworthiness.

Furthermore, you trust others only as much as you trust yourself. Start there.

11. A Leader Must Handle Resistance and Fear.

Appear fearless. Show compassion. Allow those who resist to express their fears and doubts without becoming defensive or controlling. Listen. Ask questions. Respond with empathy. You cannot allow those sitting in the parking lot outside to consume all of your precious energy, but you can't afford to write them off. With good communication, ongoing training, empowerment, and support, almost everyone will decide to join in the dance.

12. A Leader Must Be Responsible for His or Her Own Quality of Life.

How can you take care of others if you can't take care of yourself? Keep your life in balance. Your mental attitude and physical well-being must be in peak shape. Learn self-renewal techniques. If you want to succeed, take care of yourself.

PARTING THOUGHTS

There's an old Zen story about a middle-aged man who had fought his way up the corporate ladder. His marriage fell apart; he was estranged from his children, bored with his money, and physically sick.

Then someone told him there was a wise man who knew three secrets to a happy life. The man quit his job, sold his home, and began the quest to find the wise man with the secrets of happiness.

He traveled throughout the world, enduring many hardships, but at last he was rewarded. He found the wise man, sequestered high on a mountain, and knelt before him. "I have traveled a long way and endured many hardships, Master," he said. "Please tell me the three secrets of a happy life."

"Most certainly," replied the master. "The first secret of life is to pay attention."

The man was delirious. He could most certainly do that! "And what else, Master?" he begged.

"The second secret of life," said the wise Zen master, "is to pay attention."

The man could scarcely believe his ears. But the wise old master made it even clearer. He closed his eyes and said, "And the third secret of life, young man, is to pay attention."

Fritz Perls, the great pioneer of Gestalt therapy, said that most anxiety and stress is caused by "living in a dead past or an unborn future." Guilt from the past. Fear of the future.

Healing, however, is in the present.

When you begin to understand the importance and practice of being in the present, aware of the actions and the people around you, life suddenly takes on a whole new dimension.

Read the sentence in the triangle shown below:

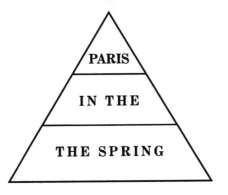

If you are like the majority of people, you read "Paris in the spring." If so, read it again, and this time, pay attention. The sentence reads, "Paris in the *the* spring."

If you saw the extra "the," congratulations. You were paying attention. Most people miss the second "the." We are conditioned to see what we expect to see, or what we want to see. The mind will try to make sense out of nonsense. Sometimes it works to our benefit, and sometimes it doesn't. Sometimes we don't see something that is very important.

> Let us not look back in anger or forward in fear but around us in awareness.
>
> —JAMES THURBER,
> American humorist

A fellow diver and I developed a different approach to scuba diving, a course called "The Zen of Diving." A Zen diver will first achieve neutral buoyancy, hanging limp and motionless, facedown in the water. Then he or she focuses his or her attention on three or four square feet of ocean floor.

At first the area may look like a lifeless piece of sand or rock, but as the diver stares, a whole world begins to open up. The sand shifts, the smallest of sea creatures emerge, colors change, and what at first appeared to be empty and lifeless becomes an absorbing, vibrant world of activity.

"The Zen of Diving" serves as a perfect metaphor. Whether you are a manager in a large corporation, a member of an office support staff, a homemaker, or an independent entrepreneur, everything comes alive when you focus on it.

Your ability to be in touch with your emotions gives you direction to make the decisions necessary to enhance your emotional well-being.

When you listen to your body's signals, you'll know when you're hungry, tired, or scared, and when you're doing the right thing.

When you learn to listen to your thoughts, you will recognize negative thoughts like shame and guilt. You can transform judgment into curiosity, criticism into suggestions, and guilt into understanding.

When you focus on others, you hear them better. Your own voice is your biggest block to listening.

When you pay attention to your surroundings, you enjoy them more. Your internal clock slows down; your natural creativity has time to be unleashed, and opportunities magically appear.

If there is one point of the Fourteen Points of Quantum Leap Thinking on which all the others depend, it is *Pay Attention*. Invisible opportunities surround us all the time. In order to see them, we have to pay attention. It is the skill with which we can develop awareness, and without which there can be no quantum leaps at all.

Once again, look at the model for Quantum Leap Thinking on the next page.

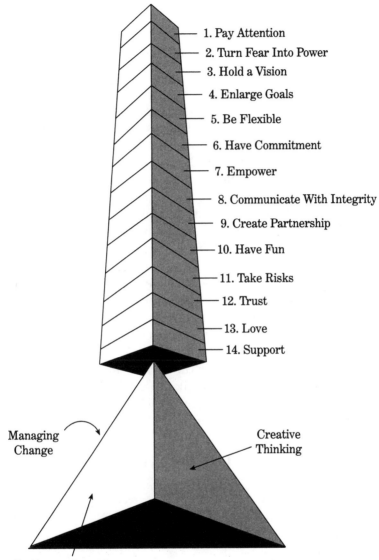

1. Pay Attention
2. Turn Fear Into Power
3. Hold a Vision
4. Enlarge Goals
5. Be Flexible
6. Have Commitment
7. Empower
8. Communicate With Integrity
9. Create Partnership
10. Have Fun
11. Take Risks
12. Trust
13. Love
14. Support

Managing Change

Creative Thinking

Continuous Learning

I wrote this book for people who want to make a difference in their own lives and the lives of those around them. When you apply the strategies presented in this model, you create your own quantum leaps. All the ingredients are there. You are the leader. You are the process.

A quantum leap is . . . the explosive jump that a particle undergoes in moving from one place to another. . . . In a figurative sense, taking the quantum leap means taking a risk, going off into an uncharted territory with no guide to follow.

—FRED ALAN WOLF,
Taking the Quantum Leap

Quantum physics, the inspiration for this book, requires us to rethink the concepts of time and space and reexamine how human consciousness operates. The model for Quantum Leap Thinking provides you with the steps that lead up to the quantum leap.

You don't have to be content with improving your life incrementally or gradually. By applying the principles of Quantum Leap Thinking, you will break the accepted mind-set that assumes success comes one step at a time. You can break the paradigm of conventional growth by stepping beyond the ordinary, the comfortable, natural, and safe, simply by the way you choose to think. You can move from your present level of achievement directly to one that is several stages higher. You can make the quantum leap, your own explosive jump that moves you far beyond the next logical step. You bring thought (waves) into reality (particle).

Quantum leaps require paradoxical thinking and behavior, unusual moves and actions that, on the surface, often seem to contradict common sense. You have to take a leap of faith.

I leave you with the following prose, which sums up my philosophy in the simplest terms possible.

IF I HAD MY LIFE TO LIVE OVER . . .

I'd like to make more mistakes next time.
I'd relax.
I would be sillier than I've been this trip.
I would take fewer things seriously.
I would take more chances.
I would eat more ice cream and less beans.
I would perhaps have more actual troubles, but I'd have fewer imaginary ones.

You see, I'm one of those people who lives sensibly and sanely, hour after hour, day after day.

Oh, I've had my moments,
And if I had it to do over again,
I'd have more of them.
In fact, I'd have nothing else,
Just moments, one after another, instead of living so many years
    ahead of each day.

I've been one of those persons who never goes anywhere without
    a thermometer, a hot water bottle, a raincoat and a parachute.
If I had it to do over again, I would travel lighter than I have.

If I had my life to live over . . .

I would start barefoot earlier in the spring, and stay that way
    later in the fall.
I would go to more dances.
I would ride more merry-go-rounds.
I would pick more daisies . . .

—NADINE STAIR,
85 years old,
Louisville, Kentucky

BIBLIOGRAPHY

Barker, Joel A. *Future Edge: Discovering the New Rules of Success.* New York: Morrow, 1992.

Belasco, James A., Ph.D. *Teaching the Elephant to Dance: Empowering Change in Your Organization.* New York: Crown Publishing Group, 1990.

Block, Peter. *The Empowered Manager: Positive Political Skills at Work.* San Francisco: Jossey-Bass, 1987.

Connellan, Thomas K. *How to Grow People Into Self Starters.* Ann Arbor, Mich.: The Achievement Institute, 1988.

Conner, Daryl R. *Managing at the Speed of Change: Guidelines for Resilience in Turbulent Times.* New York: Villard, 1993.

Covey, Stephen R. *The Seven Habits of Highly Effective People.* New York: Fireside, 1990.

De Bono, Edward. *Lateral Thinking: Creativity Step by Step.* New York: HarperCollins, 1970.

Drucker, Peter F. *The New Realities.* New York: Harper Business, 1994.

Fritz, Robert. *The Path of Least Resistance.* New York: Fawcett, 1989.

Gabor, Andrea. *The Man Who Discovered Quality: Learning to Become the Creative Force in Your Own Life.* New York: Times Books/Random House, 1990.

Garfield, Charles. *Peak Performers: The New Heroes of American Business.* New York: Avon, 1987.

Gellerman, Saul W., Ph.D. *Motivation in the Real World: The Art of Getting Extra Effort From Everyone.* New York: Dutton, 1992.

Gershon, David, and Gail Straub. *Empowerment: The Art of Creating Your Life as You Want It.* New York: Delta, 1989.

Givens, Charles J. *Super Self: Doubling Your Personal Effectiveness.* New York: Simon & Schuster, 1992.

Goldwag, Elliott M., ed. *Inner Balance: The Power of Holistic Healing.* Englewood Cliffs, N.J.: Prentice Hall, 1979.

Handy, Charles. *The Age of Unreason.* Boston: Harvard Business School Press, 1991.

Harman, Willis, Ph.D., and Howard Rheingold. *Higher Creativity.* New York: Jeremy P. Tarcher, Inc., 1984.

Herbert, Nick. *Quantum Reality: Beyond the New Physics.* New York: Anchor Press/Doubleday, 1987.

Herman, Stanley M. *A Force of Ones.* San Francisco: Jossey-Bass, 1994.

Hill, Napoleon. *Think and Grow Rich.* New York: Fawcett Crest, 1987.

Jampolsky, Gerald G., M.D. *Love Is Letting Go of Fear.* New York: Bantam, 1984.

Jeffers, Susan, Ph.D. *Feel the Fear and Do It Anyway.* New York: Harcourt Brace, 1987.

Katzenbach, Jon R., and Douglas K. Smith. *The Wisdom of Teams: Creating the High-Performance Organization.* New York: Harper Business, 1994.

Kohn, Alfie. *No Contest: The Case Against Competition.* Boston: Houghton Mifflin, 1992.

Kriegel, Robert J., and Louis Pafler. *If It Ain't Broke . . . Break It! And Other Unconventional Wisdom for a Changing Business World.* New York: Warner Books, 1991.

Leider, Richard J. *The Power of Purpose.* New York: Fawcett Gold Medal, 1985.

Leonard, George. *Mastery: The Keys to Success and Long-Term Fulfillment.* New York: Dutton, 1991.

Maltz, Maxwell, M.D. *Psycho-Cybernetics.* New York: Pocket Books, 1960.

McNally, David. *Even Eagles Need a Push: Learning to Soar in a Changing World.* Berkeley, Calif.: Transform Press, 1990.

Miller, William C. *The Creative Edge: How to Foster Innovation Where You Work.* Reading, Mass.: Addison-Wesley, 1987.

Nierenberg, Gerald I. *The Art of Creative Thinking.* New York: Simon & Schuster, 1986.

Olesen, Erik. *Twelve Steps to Mastering the Winds of Change: Peak Performers Reveal How to Stay on Top in Times of Change.* New York: Rawson Associates, 1993.

Olson, Robert W. *The Art of Creative Thinking: A Practical Guide.* Barnes & Noble, 1978.

Perkins, D. N. *The Mind's Best Work: A New Psychology of Creative Thinking.* Cambridge, Mass.: Harvard University Press, 1981.

Poppel, Ernst. *Mindworks: Time and Conscious Experience.* New York: Harcourt Brace, 1988.

Ray, Michael L., and Rochelle Meyers. *Creativity in Business.* New York: Doubleday & Company, 1986.

Reddy, W. Brendan, and Kaleel Jamison, eds. *Team Building: Blueprints for Productivity and Satisfaction.* Alexandria, Va.: NTL Institute for Applied Behavioral Science, 1988.

Robbins, Anthony. *Awaken the Giant Within: How to Take Immediate Control of Your Mental, Emotional, Physical and Financial Destiny.* New York: Fireside, 1992.

Safire, William, and Leonard Safire, eds. *Good Advice on Writing: Writers Past and Present on How to Write Well.* New York: Simon & Schuster, 1992.

Senge, Peter M. *The Fifth Discipline: Mastering the Five Practices of the Learning Organization.* New York: Doubleday, 1990.

Snyder, Neil H., and James J. Dowd, Jr. *Vision, Values and Courage: Leadership for Quality Management.* New York: The Free Press, 1994.

Tracy, Diane. *Ten Steps to Empowerment.* New York: Quill, 1992.

Wellins, Richard S., William C. Byham, and Jeanne M. Wilson. *Empowered Teams: Creating Self-Directed Work Groups That Improve Quality, Productivity and Participation.* San Francisco: Jossey-Bass, 1991.

Wells, Valerie. *The Joy of Visualization: 75 Creative Ways to Enhance Your Life.* San Francisco: Chronicle Books, 1990.

Wheatley, Margaret J. *Leadership and the New Science: Learning About Organization From an Orderly Universe.* San Francisco: Berrett-Koehler, 1994.

Wolf, Fred A. *Taking the Quantum Leap.* New York: HarperCollins, 1989.

Zohar, Danah. *The Quantum Self: A Revolutionary View of Human Nature and Consciousness Rooted in the New Physics.* New York: William Morrow and Co., 1990.

INDEX

For further information about James J. Mapes's series of audio- and videotapes, personal workshops, seminars, and corporate presentations, you may contact:

The Quantum Leap Thinking Organization
195 Sharp Hill Road
Wilton, CT 06897
Phone: 203-762-1200
Fax: 203-762-8959

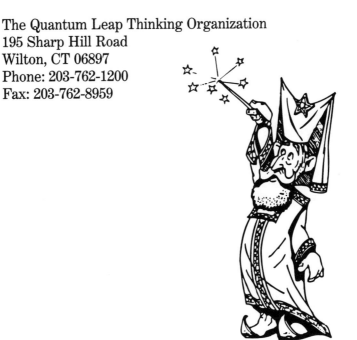